AMERICAN
HERITAGE

October 1962 · Volume XIII, Number 6

The trolley was everywhere at once: *Publishers of early post cards were not above a bit of money-saving fakery. In the three cards above, from the collection of John Ripley, the same car rolls down the same track, though the captions say otherwise. But then who—save a drummer or an interurban buff—would be likely to visit Geneva, La Porte, and Gladstone? An article on the old-time post-card craze begins on page 97.*

AMERICAN HERITAGE

The Magazine of History

PUBLISHER
James Parton
EDITORIAL DIRECTOR
Joseph J. Thorndike, Jr.
SENIOR EDITOR
Bruce Catton

EDITOR
Oliver Jensen
ASSOCIATE EDITORS
Robert Cowley
E. M. Halliday
Richard M. Ketchum
Joan Paterson Mills
Robert L. Reynolds
ASSISTANT EDITORS
Meryle Evans, Stephen W. Sears
CONTRIBUTING EDITOR
Margery Darrell
LIBRARIAN
Caroline Backlund
COPY EDITOR
Beverly Hill
ASSISTANT: Suzanne Smith

SENIOR ART DIRECTOR
Irwin Glusker
ART DIRECTOR
Murray Belsky
STAFF PHOTOGRAPHER: Herbert Loebel

ADVISORY BOARD
Allan Nevins, *Chairman*

Carl Carmer   Alvin M. Josephy, Jr.
Albert B. Corey   Richard P. McCormick
Christopher Crittenden   Harry Shaw Newman
Marshall B. Davidson   Howard H. Peckham
Louis C. Jones   S. K. Stevens
Arthur M. Schlesinger, Sr.

AMERICAN HERITAGE is published every two months by American Heritage Publishing Co., Inc., 551 Fifth Avenue, New York 17, N.Y. Correspondence about subscriptions should be addressed to: American Heritage Subscription Office, 383 West Center Street, Marion, Ohio. Single Copies: $3.95. Annual Subscriptions: $15.00 in U.S. & Canada; $16.00 elsewhere.

An annual Index of AMERICAN HERITAGE is published every February, priced at $1.00. A Cumulative Index of Volumes VI–X is available at $3.00.

AMERICAN HERITAGE will consider but assumes no responsibility for unsolicited material.
     Title registered U.S. Patent Office.
Second class postage paid at New York, N.Y., and at additional mailing offices.

Sponsored by

American Association for State & Local History · Society of American Historians

CONTENTS *October 1962 · Volume XIII, Number 6*

COVER: This painting is one of a series by Charles Wimar depicting an event which took place in dark and bloody Kentucky on July 7, 1776. The artist romanticized the scene, but the actual facts were chilling. Fourteen-year-old Jemina Boone was canoeing near Boonesborough with two friends when Indians captured them. The girls managed to mark their trail with twigs and bits of cloth ripped from their dresses, however, and three days later Boone rescued them. After fifteen years in this country the German-born Wimar returned to his homeland, to the famed academy at Dusseldorf; determined to record the life of the American Indian, he painted several scenes popularized by early U.S. historians and by novelists like James Fenimore Cooper. This canvas is owned by E. R. Minshall, Jr., of Tulsa. *Back Cover:* All that's missing in this lithograph from the collection of Mrs. Richard N. Lindaberry—the cigars in the box were called "Last Ideas"—is a cigar-box buggy.

The Farm Boy and the Angel

Of sensitive, mystical Joseph Smith, of a heavenly visitor and a buried scripture, and of the founding of a new religion destined to enlist many followers and carve from the desert a new Zion

By CARL CARMER

In the history of religion in the United States, surely no story is more astounding than that of the Mormons, or, as they style themselves, the Church of Jesus Christ of Latter-day Saints. Their chronicle has a Biblical ring, for it contains not only a revelation and a martyred prophet but also a pilgrimage through a wilderness and a discovery, after long sufferings, of a promised land. It starts with a few disciples, then a few score; today it reckons its numbers close to two millions, many of them beyond the seas, with fresh converts added daily. Yet all this is the work of barely a century and a third —as if the whole Old Testament could be crowded into the span of but four or five begats, and Moses were the contemporary of Abraham Lincoln, Ralph Waldo Emerson, and Mark Twain.

The story has its beginnings in upstate New York near the town of Palmyra, in a time of deep religious

ferment. It is told here by Carl Carmer, historian and poet, who is a member of the Council of the Society of American Historians and also of the Advisory Board of American Heritage. *In such works as* The Hudson, Listen for a Lonesome Drum, *and* Dark Trees to the Wind, *he has demonstrated his special attainments as an authority on the history and folklore of his native state. For some time now, Mr. Carmer has been engaged in research and preparation for a much-needed objective history of the Mormons. He is a "Gentile" in their terms, that is, not a Mormon, but he has been able to augment his researches through the assistance of Mormon authorities and scholars; he has pursued his studies at the Church House in Salt Lake City, at the University of Utah, and at other Mormon sources.*

This series, which begins here with the story of Joseph Smith, will continue in later issues with accounts of his violent death, of Brigham Young's trek to the shores of the Great Salt Lake, and of the establishment in Utah of the Mormon Zion. Mr. Carmer's completed manuscript, as yet untitled, will eventually be published by Doubleday. —*The Editors*

Opposite: A life-sized bronze statue of Joseph Smith stands in Salt Lake City's Temple Square, with the Mormon Temple as a backdrop. This and a companion statue of Joseph's brother, Hyrum, were executed by Mahonri Young, a grandson of the man who led the Mormons to Utah after the Smiths died.

Just after midnight had ended the twenty-first day of September in the year 1827, tall, twenty-one-year-old Joseph Smith entered the room where his mother lay and asked her if she had a chest with a lock and key. Years later Lucy Smith recounted what happened after she heard the question. She "knew in an instant what he wanted it for, and not having one, was greatly alarmed." Joseph comforted her, saying, "Never mind. I can do very well for the present without it—be calm—all is right."

The young man left his mother on her couch and strode out into the cool of the cloud-blanketed night. A moment later Emma, his tall, straight wife, "passed through the room with her bonnet and riding dress." To the mother's ears then came the familiar sounds of hitching up, and she realized at once that her son had borrowed the horse and wagon of Joseph Knight, who had arrived on a mysterious business trip from Broome County the day before, bringing with him her son's employer, farmer Josiah Stowel.

When the clopping of hooves died out, Lucy Smith began an anxious vigil filled with "prayer and supplication to God." Sleepless in the small frame farmhouse so filled with slumbering folk that it seemed itself to be breathing, she awaited the slow coming of light. In the rooms about her lay the two guests; her husband, Joseph, Sr.; and seven of her children. Twenty-seven-year-old Hyrum was her eldest now since Alvin's death three years before when he was twenty-six. Sophronia, an "old maid" at twenty-four, had at last found her man and would be married in December. Then came Samuel, nineteen; William, sixteen; Catherine, fifteen; Don Carlos, eleven; and little Lucy, six.

"At the usual hour," Lucy remembered, "I commenced preparing breakfast. My heart fluttered at every footstep as I now expected Joseph and Emma momentarily, and feared lest Joseph might meet with another disappointment."

Lucy Smith knew, as her son and his wife began their dark journey, that it was four years ago to the very night when Joseph had first seen the angel. His supernatural experience, as he had told her, had begun even earlier—when he was fourteen. At that time he had been so troubled by the bitter quarreling of proselyting evangelists in the neighboring hill-shadowed western New York town of Palmyra that he had walked alone into a grove behind his father's farmhouse and knelt in a sun-dappled sequestered place to ask God what denomination he should join. Then a pillar of light, sweeping across the treetops, came to rest before the praying boy. In it he saw two glorious beings. One of these spoke, saying that the other was His Beloved Son, and that Other told him to join no sect, but to prepare himself for a work to which he

was destined. After that, both of the beings vanished.

This event had prepared Joseph in some measure for the angel's visit to him in his little bedroom under the eaves. In his report of this, he wrote that in 1823 on the evening of the twenty-first of September as he lay in his bed praying, a light grew about him until his room was brighter than a sunny noonday. Then "a personage" appeared at his side, "standing in the air, for his feet did not touch the floor." He wore a loose robe "of most exquisite whiteness" and his hands and wrists, feet and ankles, head and neck, were bare. Since the robe was open, Joseph could see that he wore no other clothing—"his whole person was glorious beyond description and his countenance truly like lightning."

He called me by name and said unto me . . . that his name was Moroni; that God had work for me to do; and that my name should be had for good and evil among all nations, kindreds and tongues . . .

He said there was a book deposited, written upon gold plates, giving an account of the former inhabitants of this continent and the source from which they sprang. He also said that the fullness of the everlasting Gospel was contained in it, as delivered by the Saviour to the ancient inhabitants; also that there were two stones in silver bows—and these stones, fastened to a breastplate, constituted what is called the Urim and the Thummim—deposited with the plates; and the possession and use of these stones were what constituted "Seers" in ancient or former times; and that God had prepared them for the purpose of translating the book.

Moroni delivered his message three times that night. On his second appearance the angel added that the plates and the seer-stone spectacles must not be shown, except to those persons to whom the Lord commanded they be revealed. "While he was conversing," wrote Joseph, ". . . the vision was opened to my mind that I could see the place where the plates were deposited, and that so clearly and distinctly that I knew the place again when I visited it." On his third visit Moroni warned the boy that he "must have no object in getting the plates but to glorify God."

Each time, as the angel messenger departed, Joseph said, he saw, "as it were, a conduit open right up into heaven, and he ascended until he had entirely disappeared." After this had happened for the third time, the Smith rooster crowed, and the boy, weakened by his experience, realized he must get up at once and begin the labor of a new day.

Working with his father that morning Joseph found himself so exhausted that he could not go on. The older man observed "something wrong" and told his son to go back to the house. As he tried to climb the fence at the edge of the field, he fell helpless to the ground, and again the familiar figure of Moroni, standing above him, bade him go to his father and tell

THE

BOOK OF MORMON:

AN ACCOUNT WRITTEN BY THE HAND OF MOR-
MON, UPON PLATES TAKEN FROM
THE PLATES OF NEPHI.

Wherefore it is an abridgment of the Record of the People of Nephi; and also of the Lamanites; written to the Lamanites, which are a remnant of the House of Israel; and also to Jew and Gentile; written by way of commandment, and also by the spirit of Prophesy and of Revelation. Written, and sealed up, and hid up unto the LORD, that they might not be destroyed; to come forth by the gift and power of GOD unto the interpretation thereof; sealed by the hand of Moroni, and hid up unto the LORD, to come forth in due time by the way of Gentile; the interpretation thereof by the gift of GOD; an abridgment taken from the Book of Ether.

Also, which is a Record of the People of Jared, which were scattered at the time the LORD confounded the language of the people when they were building a tower to get to Heaven: which is to shew unto the remnant of the House of Israel how great things the LORD hath done for their fathers; and that they may know the covenants of the LORD, that they are not cast off forever; and also to the convincing of the Jew and Gentile that JESUS is the CHRIST, the ETERNAL GOD, manifesting Himself unto all nations. And now if there be fault, it be the mistake of men: wherefore condemn not the things of GOD, that ye may be found spotless at the judgment seat of CHRIST.

BY JOSEPH SMITH, JUNIOR,

AUTHOR AND PROPRIETOR.

PALMYRA:

PRINTED BY E. B. GRANDIN, FOR THE AUTHOR.

1830.

PREFACE.

To THE READER—

As many false reports have been circulated respecting the following work, and also many unlawful measures taken by evil designing persons to destroy me, and also the work, I would inform you that I translated, by the gift and power of God, and caused to be written, one hundred and sixteen pages, the which I took from the Book of Lehi, which was an account abridged from the plates of Lehi, by the hand of Mormon; which said account, some person or persons have stolen and kept from me, notwithstanding my utmost exertions to recover it again—and being commanded of the Lord that I should not translate the same over again, for Satan had put it into their hearts to tempt the Lord their God, by altering the words, that they did read contrary from that which I translated and caused to be written; and if I should bring forth the same words again, or, in other words, if I should translate the same over again, they would publish that which they had stolen, and Satan would stir up the hearts of this generation, that they might not receive this work: but behold, the Lord said unto me, I will not suffer that Satan shall accomplish his evil design in this thing: therefore thou shalt translate from the plates of Nephi, until ye come to that which ye have translated, which ye have retained; and

behold ye shall publish it as the record of Nephi; and thus I will confound those who have altered my words. I will not suffer that they shall destroy my work; yea, I will shew unto them that my wisdom is greater than the cunning of the Devil. Wherefore, to be obedient unto the commandments of God, I have, through his grace and mercy, accomplished that which he hath commanded me respecting this thing. I would also inform you that the plates of which hath been spoken, were found in the township of Manchester, Ontario county, New-York.

THE AUTHOR.

AND ALSO THE TESTIMONY OF EIGHT WITNESSES.

BE it known unto all nations, kindreds, tongues, and people, unto whom this work shall come, that Joseph Smith, Jr. the Author and Proprietor of this work, has shewn unto us the plates of which hath been spoken, which have the appearance of gold; and as many of the leaves as the said Smith has translated, we did handle with our hands; and we also saw the engravings thereon, all of which has the appearance of ancient work, and of curious workmanship. And this we bear record, with words of soberness, that the said Smith has shewn unto us, for we have seen and hefted, and know of a surety, that the said Smith has got the plates of which we have spoken. And we give our names unto the world, to witness unto the world that which we have seen: and we lie not, God bearing witness of it.

CHRISTIAN WHITMER,
JACOB WHITMER,
PETER WHITMER, JR.
JOHN WHITMER,
HIRAM PAGE,
JOSEPH SMITH, SEN.
HYRUM SMITH,
SAMUEL H. SMITH.

THE BOOK OF MORMON

The golden plates (see Smith's drawing of three lines, below) that Joseph Smith unearthed on Hill Cumorah in 1823 he later translated into The Book of Mormon, first published in 1830. This and the Christian Bible ("as far as it is translated correctly") the Mormons believe to be divinely inspired. They also believe that Jesus is the Son of God and that He established "the Church of Jesus Christ." But they hold that shortly after the death of His original apostles, widespread apostasy set in and divine guidance of the Church ceased—until Peter, James, John, and John the Baptist returned to earth and ordained Joseph Smith to re-establish the Church of Jesus Christ. Thus the Mormons are Christians, but neither Protestants nor Roman Catholics (whose church they believe started when the great schism of 1054 divided Western and Eastern churches).

Three pages from a first edition of The Book of Mormon are reproduced above. The title page lists Joseph Smith as both "Author" and "Proprietor." (Modern editions call him merely "translator.") Smith's Preface recounts the losing by farmer Martin Harris, who financed publication of the book, of 116 pages of the original translation. The "testimony" reproduced at right is still carried, along with another supporting statement by Harris, Oliver Cowdery, and David Whitmer, in every edition; several of the witnesses left the church at one time or another, and four died outside it, but all except Page reaffirmed their testimony before they died.

In essence The Book of Mormon is a history of two peoples supposed to have inhabited America in ancient times. The Jaredites, it relates, were Israelites whom God led out of the confusion of the Tower of Babel and across the oceans to America, where internal dissensions eventually brought about their extermination, near the Hill Cumorah, about 590 B.C. About the same time, Mormons believe, followers of a Jewish prophet, Lehi, landed on the western coast of America. They subsequently split into two factions—the civilized Nephites and the savage Lamanites, ancestors of the American Indians. In a climactic struggle about 400 A.D.—near the Hill Cumorah—the Lamanites destroyed the Nephites, whose last survivors were the prophet Mormon and his son Moroni. They, Smith asserted, abridged and recorded the secular and ecclesiastical history of these peoples on plates which, centuries later, the resurrected Moroni delivered to him.

of his vision and of the commandments he had received. When he could rise again Joseph obeyed the angel, and the senior Joseph Smith told him that the orders of the messenger must be carried out. This matter, said the father, was of God.

Despite fatigue of mind and body, Joseph plodded up the slope of the nearby hill on which the angel had revealed that the golden plates and the magic spectacles lay. As he neared the summit, he was amazed that he recognized every detail of the place from his clairvoyant vision of the night before.

Convenient to the village of Manchester, Ontario County, New York stands a hill of considerable size, and the most elevated of any in the neighborhood. On the west side of this hill, not far from the top, under a stone of considerable size, lay the plates deposited in a stone box. This stone was thick and rounding in the middle on the upper side, and thinner towards the edges, so that the middle part of it was visible above the ground, but the edge all round was covered with earth.

Having removed the earth, I obtained a lever, which I got fixed under the edge of the stone and with a little exertion raised it up. I looked in, and there indeed I did behold the plates, the Urim and Thummim, and the breastplate, as stated by the messenger. The box in which they lay was formed by laying stones together in some kind of cement. In the bottom of the box were laid two stones crossways of the box, and on these stones lay the plates and the other things with them.

Eagerly Joseph worked the top rock aside and bent over to lift the discovered treasures. And immediately Moroni, "the messenger sent from the presence of God," was with him for the fifth time, saying sternly that the moment for removing these things was not yet, "but he told me I should come to that place precisely one year from that time and that he would there meet with me, and that I should continue to do so until the time should come for obtaining the plates."

On the evening of that day Joseph sat up late, informing his family of the new revelations told by the angel. He was so weary, however, that at the suggestion of his brother Alvin all agreed to rise early the next morning and to finish the next day's work an hour before sunset. Early supper would then allow a long evening for hearing Joseph's report. And so, when sunset came again, the boy continued his story, first warning his family that what he told them must be held secret. The world, he said, was so wicked that they would be persecuted, perhaps murdered, if they told these things to their neighbors. From that time on, the parents continued getting the children together after supper to hear the instructions which Joseph said he was receiving from the Lord. His mother wrote of these evenings years later: "I presume

our family presented an aspect as singular as any that ever lived upon the face of the earth—all seated in a circle, father, mother, sons and daughters, and giving the most profound attention to a boy, eighteen years of age, who had never read the Bible through in his life; he seemed much less inclined to the perusal of books than any of the rest of our children, but far more given to meditation and deep study."

It was this same boy, grown to manhood and recently married to brown-eyed Emma Hale, who, with his bride on the wagon seat beside him, drove Joseph Knight's horse to the foot of the familiar hill on the anniversary night of September 21, 1827. There is no record of his meetings with the angel of the hill in the intervening years, save his statements that they took place and that on each occasion he received additional instructions. Nor is there any account other than hearsay of what happened at this reunion when the angel was to fulfill his promise. Believers think it logical to assume that Joseph left Emma in the wagon at the foot of the slope and took his accustomed path to the west side of the summit. There, according to his tell, Moroni awaited him. Since later companions beheld the holy light that surrounded supernatural beings appearing before them, Emma might have claimed to have seen the glow on the hill where her husband spoke with the angel. If so, she did not describe it.

Moroni, Joseph wrote later, directed him to take the contents of the stone box but charged him that he should be responsible for them and should not carelessly let them go on pain of his being "cut off." The angel said that he would call for these treasures when he wished them returned, and he bade Joseph to preserve and protect them.

Although Joseph's mother could not provide a chest for the golden plates, he may have found one or obtained a substitute that would hide them from human sight. Six years later, one Fayette Lapham, a neighbor, is reported to have claimed that Joseph's father said his son carried the plates down the hill in a chest which was concealed in a pillow-slip. If, as one of the ablest Mormon historians, B. H. Roberts, deduces, neither Emma nor Lucy Smith was aware, on that morning after Joseph returned home, of his actual possession of the golden record, he must have hidden it before returning to the wagon. Fayette Lapham said that according to Father Smith's tell, a host of devils, yelling hideously, met Joseph as he climbed a fence on his downward journey, and one of them struck him so hard that "a black and blue spot remained for three or four days." Joseph did not ever mention these devils. He said only that he hid the plates in a hollow birch log lying in the woods two or three miles from his home. The walk from the bottom of the hill to this place must have been long, and it is not surprising that Lucy Smith did not hear the sounds of the horse and wagon until after she had served breakfast.

At the sight of her son she was so unnerved that, fearing his mission had been unsuccessful, she left the room. Joseph understood and followed her.

"Do not be uneasy, Mother," he said kindly, "all is right—see here, I have got a key."

Apparently his mind had raced beyond Lucy's to the problem of translating the plates, while she still worried over whether or not he had obtained them. He then held out to his mother the gleaming spectacles, Urim and Thummim, the "key" by which he would be enabled to translate the golden record he had hidden in the hollow birch. Lucy took them in her hand and saw them as "two smooth, three-cornered diamonds set in glass and the glasses set in silver bows." With them was a breastplate which her son had wrapped in a muslin handkerchief. "It was concave on one side and convex on the other," she wrote, "and extended from the neck downwards as far as the center of the stomach of a man of extraordinary size."

This article she might well have expected to behold from reading her Bible. A breastplate is coupled with Urim and Thummim in two of the seven books of the Old Testament in which they are named. They seem to have been designated as aids in obtaining understandable guidance from the Lord when He has been formally petitioned. Exodus records the detailed instructions given to Moses by the Lord for the making of Aaron's "breastplate of judgment," which was to be "of gold, of silver, of blue and of purple, and of scarlet, and of fine twined linen," and was to contain four rows of three stones each arranged as follows: sardius, topaz, and carbuncle; emerald, sapphire, and diamond; ligure, agate, and amethyst; beryl, onyx, and jasper. "And thou shalt put in the breastplate of judgment," said the Lord, "the Urim and the Thummim; and they shall be upon Aaron's heart when he goeth in before the Lord." Moses, according to Leviticus, obeyed—

"And he put the breastplate upon him: also he put in the breastplate the Urim and the Thummim."

After Joseph had hidden the magic spectacles in the house he told the miraculous news to all present.

The finding of the golden book did not remain a secret. Lucy Smith told a close friend in strict confidence, and the news traveled with amazing speed about the whole community. Jealousy rather than incredulity was the immediate reaction. Neighbor Willard Chase, a Methodist "class-leader," was so overwhelmed with envy that he at once sent for a noted clairvoyant living some sixty miles away. So urgent was the message that the psychic rode all of a night and a day to arrive in time for a conference at the Chase home, where he swore, "we will have them plates in spite of Joe Smith or all the devils in hell."

In the meantime Joseph had accepted a job. A man named Warner had brought him a message from the widow Wells in nearby Macedon. She wished Joseph to come and mend her well. Since, as his mother said, "there was not a shilling in the house," this was a welcome assignment, and her son set out at once.

SULTNER-WELLES

By the next morning the excitement in the country about Palmyra was so great that the Smith family feared immediate action would be taken to find and seize the hidden treasure. Emma volunteered to ride to Macedon to bring back her husband.

Upon the return of the young couple to the Smith house, they found the senior Joseph Smith pacing nervously back and forth, and Joseph said, "Father, there is no danger—all is perfectly safe —there is no cause for alarm."

He sent his youngest brother, Don Carlos, to tell brother Hyrum to come at once. Hyrum arrived, and Joseph told him to get a chest with a lock and key—and have it ready by the time he returned with the golden plates.

CONTINUED ON PAGE 80

The Mormon monument, a forty-foot shaft capped by a statue of the Angel Moroni, stands atop Hill Cumorah, a glacial drumlin near Manchester in northwestern New York State. This is the Mormons' Mount Sinai: here, in 1823, Joseph Smith said he found the golden plates he translated into the Book of Mormon.

9

FACES FROM THE PAST—VIII

"The most damnable outrage ever!" the Memphis *Scimitar* called it. President Theodore Roosevelt, it was learned, had entertained a black man at dinner at the White House, and the reaction was about what might have been expected in America in 1901. One southern newspaper described the affair as "a crime equal to treason"; an editor warned that "no Southern woman with proper respect would now accept an invitation to the White House." And "Pitchfork Ben" Tillman, the irascible, one-eyed, unsuccessful farmer who was now a senator from South Carolina, spoke for the militant racists: "Entertaining that nigger," he said, would "necessitate our killing a thousand niggers in the South before they will learn their place again."

The object of this furor was a forty-five-year-old, mild-mannered gentleman who had been a slave until about the age of nine. The son of a Negro cook and an unknown father—possibly a white man from a neighboring plantation—he was born in "the most miserable, desolate, and discouraging surroundings" on James Burroughs' plantation in Franklin County, Virginia. With his mother and two other children he lived in a fourteen-by-sixteen cabin which had an open fireplace, a door, several uncovered openings in the walls, and a potato-hole in the middle of the dirt floor, where vegetables were stored. He couldn't recall ever sitting down to a meal with his family; slave children simply picked up scraps of bread or meat whenever they could, and often he breakfasted on boiled corn that the pigs had left on the ground around the trough. His first shoes were made of wood, and he remembered with horror the flax shirts he had to wear—before you broke them in, it was like having "a dozen or more chestnut burrs, or a hundred small pin-points" next to your skin. Equally memorable was his first glimpse of a school; he had walked as far as the schoolhouse door, carrying books for one of his young mistresses, and, looking inside and seeing several dozen boys and girls studying, imagined it to be "about the same as getting into paradise."

His first realization that he was a slave came early one morning when he awoke to find his mother kneeling over her children, praying that Mr. Lincoln and his armies would be successful so that she and the little ones might be free. For years the Negro grapevine had passed along the presentiments of freedom—the words of Garrison and Lovejoy, Brown and Lincoln—and late at night in the slave quarters there would be whispered discussions about events far to the northward. Slavery was what the war was about, they knew, and Union victory would mean the end of slavery. During the spring of 1865 freedom was in the air, and as the great day drew closer there was more singing in the slave huts than ever—bolder songs, with more of a ring to them. One momentous morning all the slaves gathered around the veranda of the big house while a stranger—a U.S. Army officer—made a little speech and read the Emancipation Proclamation. When the boy turned to his mother he saw tears of joy streaming down her cheeks.

For a time there was rejoicing, but when they returned to the cabins the boy saw a change come over the Negroes: "The great responsibility of being free, of having charge of themselves, of having to think and plan for themselves and their children, seemed to take possession of them." And in the months to come he learned more about the demands liberty makes upon people. He saw, among other things, a whole race beginning to go to school for the first time (many of the older folk so they might learn to read the Bible before they died). He went to work in a salt furnace, starting at 4 A.M. so that he might get to school by nine. And here for the first time the boy acquired a name—always he had been called Booker, but when the teacher asked for a surname he had to make one up: "Washington," he announced proudly. Not until later did he discover that his mother had named him Taliaferro, but Washington was his choice, and as Booker Taliaferro Washington he worked his way through Hampton Institute, taught school (children by day and adults at night), and in 1881 was asked to take charge of what was to be a normal school for Negroes in Tuskegee, Alabama. There was not much there to begin with—"a broken-down shanty and an old hen-house" in such bad repair that one of the students had to hold an umbrella over their teacher when it rained—but by the time he died in 1915 the institution owned nearly thirty thousand acres of land, one hundred buildings (many built by the students), had an endowment of two million dollars, and was teaching thirty-eight trades and professions. "I want to see education as common as grass, and as free for all as sunshine and rain," Washington once said, and in this belief he plunged ahead, making Tuskegee an institution that commanded the respect and support of an entire community—and eventually of the nation—by providing what the community needed.

To some Negroes of his own day—and to many a half-century later—"Booker T." seemed as out-of-date as his collar, a subservient "Uncle Tom," willing to bow before the Jim Crow laws which came in during the latter part of his life. The young N.A.A.C.P. criticized his failure to push for political rights and his emphasis on industrial education; might that not keep the race in a new bondage? But Washington left no doubts about his philosophy: he was more interested in making his race worthy of the vote than in agitating for it. He believed they would be granted it some day, and he wanted them to be ready when the great day came.

He could be patient with both races—as he demonstrated after the storm broke over his visit to the White House. "It is the smaller, the petty things in life that divide people," he observed. "It is the great tasks that bring men together."

—*Richard M. Ketchum*

No matter what the record books seem to say, John F. Kennedy was not elected President of the United States on November 8, 1960, by 34,221,485 votes over Richard M. Nixon's 34,108,684. On that Election Day, 1960, John F. Kennedy merely won a popularity contest.

He was elected President on December 19, 1960, by 303 votes over Nixon's 219.

He could have won the November popularity contest and still have lost the December election to his opponent. That has happened—to Grover Cleveland in 1888, for example.

He could have won the November popularity contest, missed election in December by getting fewer than the 269 votes he needed (albeit more than his nearest rival), and lost the Presidency in January to Nixon. That, too, has happened, a couple of times. (In 1876 Democrat Samuel J. Tilden won the November election by 264,292 votes, missed the December canvass by one vote, and eventually saw his Republican rival, Rutherford B. Hayes, inaugurated as President.)

Finally, Kennedy could have won the November

contest, missed the December election by one or more votes, and seen his running mate, Lyndon B. Johnson, take the oath as President in his stead. *That* hasn't quite happened in our history (though something like it very nearly did), but it could have this time. There were a number of consequential persons, including the governor of a sovereign state and editors of important newspapers, who were trying to make it happen. The constitutional and statutory conditions were favorable. Practical political considerations happened not to be.

On some future occasion they may be. It is pure luck that keeps things from going far awry under what is at best a caricature of democratic process. By reason of this system, the President and Vice President remain the only elective officials of the United States not chosen by direct vote of the people (a distinction senators shared with them until 1913).

The Electoral College, an American political curiosity, is established in Article II, Section I of the Constitution as revised, but only dubiously improved, by the Twelfth and Twentieth Amendments. The Electors "appointed" by the voters in their ballots on Election Day meet in their state capitals on "the first Monday after the second Wednesday in December next following their appointment" to elect the President and Vice President by two separate ballots. Their choice need not be that indicated by the voters in November. The two men they select need not even be of the same party.

Should a majority of the Electors fail to agree on any one candidate for President, then the choice devolves upon the House of Representatives, or (for Vice President in a similar case) upon the Senate. That is part of the clue to how Lyndon Johnson might have become President. The other part is that the Electors, once appointed, are completely free to vote as they wish, for any native-born man—or woman—over thirty-five years of age, or for no one. It is their prerogative under the Constitution—it is their duty by the design of the framers of the Constitution—to vote as their judgment dictates. It fails to be diminished by any

St. Paul, December 19, 1960: In a purely ritualistic election, Minnesota's "appointed" Electors (actually representatives of the popular majority in that state) choose Kennedy.

It nearly put Burr in the saddle in 1800
Choose the Best Man?

By HARRY LOUIS SELDEN

the people's choice in 1824, 1876, and 1888

It could have ditched Kennedy in 1960

party pledge they may have given or any party "loyalty oath" they may have taken. No legal means exist to compel them to observe such a pledge, or to punish them if they break it—as some have done from time to time, including the year 1960.

Since the number of Electors is equal to the total of senators and representatives, which was 537 in 1960, the majority needed to elect was 269. The Electoral College cast 300 votes each for Messrs. Kennedy and Johnson and elected them; 219 each for Messrs. Nixon and Lodge; and 15 for Harry F. Byrd with 14 vice presidential ballots for J. Strom Thurmond and one for Barry Goldwater. (Hawaii's three votes were still in question that day, but they were not material to the outcome. They were eventually cast for Kennedy and Johnson.)

The Kennedy-Johnson votes came from states in which the popularity contest gave them a plurality, no matter how slender. With one exception, they received *all* of the electoral votes from these states. With one exception, the Nixon-Lodge ticket received *all* the electoral votes of every state whose voters gave them the edge, no matter how slight.

The first exception was Alabama, where six of the eleven Democratic Electors voted for Byrd and Thurmond, although the Kennedy ticket won more than fifty-six per cent of the popular vote. The other was Oklahoma, in which the Nixon ticket received fifty-nine per cent of the popular vote but one Elector cast a motley Byrd-Goldwater ballot. Byrd's and Thurmond's remaining electoral votes came from Mississippi's eight Electors, who had proclaimed their insurgency and voting intentions from the beginning, so that the people presumably knew whom they were voting for on November 8.

Between November 8 and December 19, these rebellious Electors, including the Governor of Mississippi, made energetic efforts in other southern states to persuade their colleagues to exercise their Constitution-given prerogative to vote independently of the electorate's indicated wishes. Had they prevailed

on only thirty-five to withhold their presidential votes from Kennedy (whether or not they gave them to Byrd), no one candidate would have received a majority.

Immediately—the Constitution's word—upon formally learning of this situation after it convened on January 6, 1961, the House of Representatives would have had to go into session to try to elect a Chief Executive. The constitutional rules governing this contingency require election by a majority of all the states, each state casting one vote, as decided by the majority of its delegation in the House.

The House lineup of states on that day was: Democratic majority in the delegation, 29 states; Republican majority, 17; tied, 4. On a straight party division, then, Mr. Kennedy could have been elected in the House (limited in its choice to the leading contenders "not exceeding three"). But if the congressional delegations of four or more states had followed the lead of the rebellious Electors and refused Mr. Kennedy their votes, he would not have had a majority of the fifty states and would not have been elected. Mr. Nixon could have won only if nine Democratic states had

Washington, January 6, 1961: Escorted by senators and Vice President Nixon, Senate page boys carry boxes of electoral ballots to a joint session of Congress for official counting.

13

joined the seventeen Republican states to vote for him —a most unlikely development.

There would thus have been a stalemate. The rules would have kept the House voting, but if the four "anti-Kennedy" states had held out, the deadlock would have remained unbroken.

Now let us examine the situation with respect to the Vice Presidency. Our "rebelling" southern Electors might also have withheld their second-place ballots from Lyndon Johnson of Texas. In that case, the election of Vice President would have fallen to the Senate. Here a majority of all the senators, one vote per man, is needed to elect, with the choice restricted to the two top contenders. As there were 64 Democratic and 36 Republican senators, it is unlikely that Senator

Johnson could have failed of election. Fourteen Democratic senators would have had to go on record against him to deprive him of a majority.

Now we have Lyndon B. Johnson elected Vice President, a stalemate for President, and January 20 approaching. The Twentieth Amendment prescribes that "if a President shall not have been chosen before the time fixed for the beginning of his term . . . then the Vice President elect shall act as President until a President shall have qualified." And that would have depended on how long the recalcitrant congressmen held out; it could have been to the end of their term—two years, and then two more, if they were re-elected. At any rate, on January 20, 1961, Lyndon Johnson would have been sworn in as President, and Senator Kennedy

TEXT CONTINUES ON PAGE 18

Thomas Prichard Rossiter's depiction of the Constitutional Convention of 1787 (above) suggests the intellectual and social climate that gave rise to the Electoral College: a distrust of the common people by a well-born, educated elite. By contrast, George Caleb Bingham's 1855 painting The Verdict of the People (below) evokes the popular view of elections as democratic folk festivals.

THE
FLORIDA CASE—
BEFORE THE
ELECTORAL
COMMISSION

*see key
on page 19*

would have been sitting with the other senators, looking on.

When South Carolina's Electoral College convened on December 19, its chairman spoke of the "crackpot correspondence" he and others had received urging their defection. He expressed the hope that "you haven't been influenced by it." His colleagues hadn't, nor had any other Electors—with the exceptions already noted—in 1960. Political discretion dictated a wiser course. But if in 1860 it was conceivable that eleven states should secede from the Union against *all* political discretion, it is not inconceivable that in some not-too-distant election a group of Electors might see power or coercive advantage in this sort of maneuver.

In 1876, the strange workings of the electoral system were to bring the nation closer to civil war than it appeared to be in 1861 the day before Fort Sumter was attacked. With Tilden 264,292 popular votes ahead of Hayes and one disputed vote short of victory in the Electoral College, Congress ducked behind a wholly extra-constitutional device—an "Electoral Commission" —to solve an ugly dilemma. The atmosphere was such, wrote the historian Paul L. Haworth, that "probably more people dreaded an armed conflict than had anticipated a like outcome to the secession movement of 1860–61." Only Tilden's aloofness from the strife, and lavish promises made on Hayes' behalf by his supporters, prevented an unhappy end when the commission, by a vote of eight to seven, chose Hayes. (The story of the Hayes-Tilden election is told in "The Election That Got Away," AMERICAN HERITAGE, October, 1960.) Installed in office, Hayes made good on his promises to the Democrats, which included withdrawal of federal troops and carpetbagger governments from those southern states in which they still remained. But nothing was done to insure against a recurrence of the near-shambles of that presidential election.

Supreme Court Justice Joseph P. Bradley, the Electoral Commissioner who cast the deciding vote that gave Hayes the Presidency, bitterly termed the Electors "party puppets." As far back as 1823, Thomas Hart Benton, senator from Missouri, declared that "every reason which induced the [Constitutional] convention to institute Electors has failed. They are no longer of any use, and may be dangerous to the liberties of the people."

The chief reason which induced the delegates to the Constitutional Convention of 1787 to institute Electors was a distrust of democracy held by many of them. A sparse handful (Benjamin Franklin, John Dickinson, Gouverneur Morris, James Wilson) argued for popular election of the Executive. But the greater

number held with Roger Sherman that "the people at large" could never be "sufficiently informed" to make a proper choice. To leave it to the people would be as "unnatural," scoffed George Mason, "as it would be to refer a trial of colors to a blind man." Elbridge Gerry (later to devise the cynical "gerrymander" to give his party numerical advantage in the Massachusetts legislature) was not merely patronizing; he believed the evils of the times flowed "from the excess of democracy."

But if the Founding Fathers were thus contemptuous of *popular* democracy, they were enamored of *representative* democracy. There is no paradox here if we understand that "representation" in their comprehension was not direct and instructed, but "virtual" and paternalistic, as in England. Elected legislators were considered to represent the interests not only of the gentry who elected them, but also of the "great unwashed" (as Edmund Burke first termed them) and of the unfranchised in their constituencies.

Dedicated to the principle of representative democracy on these terms, and to its corollary of legislative supremacy, the majority of the delegates voted first and last for appointment of the national Executive by Congress. Between first and last, they let themselves be persuaded to consider, and even adopt briefly, a dozen different methods. At the same time they tussled over the troublesome problems of how many persons the Executive should comprise, its tenure, re-eligibility, powers, and prerogatives. Discussion of each problem led to fresh consideration of the method of appointment, and construction of this part of the Constitution took more time and involved more debate than all the rest together. In the end the Fathers reverted to their original instinct: appointment of the President (as he was by now called) by the Congress.

But it wasn't quite the end, as it turned out. A committee now took over the chore of polishing the rough product the Convention had fashioned. On the committee sat Gouverneur Morris, who had argued that under the plan decided on, the Executive would be the "mere creature" of the Congress; that this method would "result in executive dependence, and consequently in legislative usurpation and tyranny, as happened in England in the last century." (He referred to the Cromwell protectorate.)

With him was James Madison, who had opposed legislative appointment because it did violence to his cherished doctrine of separation of powers. Together, Morris and Madison persuaded their colleagues to adopt the plan used by Maryland for electing its state senators—a body of electors. Each state would have as many Electors as it had senators and representatives, appointed "in such manner as the Legislature

CONTINUED ON PAGE 92

The Florida Case—Before the Electoral Commission

(Painting reproduced on pages 16 and 17)

In February, 1877, members of both houses of Congress, a specially chosen Electoral Commission, and privileged visitors all crowded into the Supreme Court Chamber to hear argument over the counting of electoral votes for the disputed Tilden-Hayes election. The amazing painting by Cornelia Adele Fassett, showing more than 200 recognizable portraits of well-known Americans of the period, dramatizes the intense debate occasioned by the fact that the electoral return from Florida had been challenged by a second set of electoral votes from the same state. Eminent counsel had been retained by both Republicans and Democrats to present arguments for the certification of their respective Electors. The commission (seated in a row on the rostrum, beneath the press gallery) decided by a vote of eight to seven to certify the Republican Electors; and after similar decisions for several other disputed states, the official electoral count went to Hayes, 185 to 184, despite his minority in the popular vote. The key below identifies 64 of the most noteworthy figures, many of whom sat individually as models for the artist over a period of some two years.

On the rostrum (All members of the Electoral Commission):

1. Allen G. Thurman, senator from Ohio; **2.** Thomas F. Bayard, senator from Delaware, Secretary of State under Cleveland; **3.** Frederick T. Frelinghuysen, senator from New Jersey, Secretary of State under Arthur; **4.** Oliver P. Morton, senator from Indiana, Civil War governor; **5.** George F. Edmunds, senator from Vermont; **6.** William Strong, Supreme Court Justice; **7.** Samuel F. Miller, Supreme Court Justice; **8.** Nathan Clifford, Supreme Court Justice, formerly Attorney General under Polk; **9.** Stephen J. Field, Supreme Court Justice, brother of Cyrus; **10.** Joseph P. Bradley, Supreme Court Justice; **11.** Henry B. Payne, representative from Ohio; **12.** Eppa Hunton, representative from Virginia; **13.** Josiah G. Abbott, representative from Massachusetts; **14.** James A. Garfield, representative from Ohio, later President; **15.** George Hoar, Massachusetts representative.

On the main floor:

16. Francis Kernan, senator from New York; **17.** Lucius Quintus Cincinnatus Lamar, representative from Mississippi, later Justice of the U.S. Supreme Court; **18.** John B. Gordon, senator from Georgia, Confederate general; **19.** John A. Logan, senator from Illinois, Union general; **20.** Hannibal Hamlin, senator from Maine and Lincoln's first Vice President; **21.** George Bancroft, famed historian; **22.** William W. Corcoran, founder of the Corcoran Gallery; **23.** John H. Reagan, representa-

tive from Texas, formerly a Confederate Postmaster General and Secretary of Treasury; **24.** Justin S. Morrill, senator from Vermont and sponsor of land-grant colleges; **25.** Thomas W. Ferry, president *pro tem* of the Senate; **26.** James D. Cameron, Secretary of War, later senator from Pennsylvania; **27.** David Dudley Field, representative from New York, chief counsel for Tilden, and brother of Cyrus and Stephen No. 9 above; **28.** Roscoe Conkling, senator from New York; **29.** Montgomery Blair, counsel for Tilden, Postmaster General under Lincoln; **30.** John Sherman, senator from Ohio, later Secretary of Treasury under Hayes, and of State under McKinley, brother of General William T. Sherman; **31.** George W. McCrary, representative from Iowa, counsel for Hayes, later his Secretary of War; **32.** Morrison R. Waite, Chief Justice of the U.S. Supreme Court; **33.** John G. Nicolay, marshal of the U.S. Supreme Court, former secretary and biographer of Lincoln; **34.** Joseph Henry, physicist and first director of the Smithsonian Institution; **35.** Hamilton Fish, Secretary of State; **36.** Stephen A. Hurlbut, representative from Illinois, Union general; **37.** Stanley Matthews, counsel for Hayes, Justice of the U.S. Supreme Court; **38.** Mrs. Julia G. Tyler, widow of the former President of the U.S.; **39.** Mrs. James A. Garfield; **40.** William M. Evarts, chief counsel for Hayes, later his Secretary of State; **41.** Alphonso Taft, Attorney General, father of future President William Howard Taft; **42.** William E. Chandler, counsel for Hayes, Secretary of the Navy under Arthur; **43.**

Belva Lockwood, lawyer and first woman candidate for the Presidency; **44.** George S. Boutwell, senator from Massachusetts, Secretary of the Treasury under Grant; **45.** James N. Tyner, Postmaster General; **46.** Zachariah Chandler, Secretary of the Interior; **47.** Abram S. Hewitt, representative from New York, later Mayor of New York City; **48.** Mathew B. Brady, Civil War photographer; **49.** Ambrose E. Burnside, senator from Rhode Island, Union general; **50.** Samuel J. Randall, Speaker of the House of Representatives; **51.** Francis M. Cockrell, senator from Missouri, Confederate general; **52.** Fernando Wood, representative from New York, formerly Mayor of New York City; **53.** Thomas Ewing, representative from Ohio, Union general; **54.** Nathaniel P. Banks, representative from Massachusetts, former governor, and Union general; **55.** Joseph Gurney Cannon, representative from Illinois and later Speaker of the House; **56.** John Wesley Powell of the U.S. Geological Survey, famed explorer of the Colorado River; **57.** Frederick Douglass, famous Negro leader; **58.** Lyman Trumbull, counsel for Tilden; **59.** Jeremiah S. Black, counsel for Tilden, Attorney General and Secretary of State under Buchanan; **60.** Mrs. Cornelia Adele Fassett, the artist; **61.** James G. Blaine, senator from Maine and 1884 G.O.P. presidential candidate; **62.** Blanche K. Bruce, senator from Mississippi, a Negro; **63.** J. Randolph Tucker, representative from Virginia, counsel for Tilden; **64.** Henry Watterson, representative from Kentucky, and editor of Louisville *Courier-Journal*.

By JAMES THOMAS FLEXNER

THE DARK WORLD of DAVID GILMOUR BLYTHE

Blythe, a self-portrait

In an age when art radiated nothing but light and optimism, this self-taught painter from Pittsburgh saw another, more somber side of American life

As the raft on which she drifted carried her down the half-tamed Ohio, Susan Blythe envisioned bright futures for the child that stirred within her. If the destiny of any emerging life were in truth unpredictable, surely, here in a world of huge skies and endless resources, the auguries were good. It was to find these auguries that she and her Scottish husband had adventured from her native Ireland. Far from Europe's ancient, killing winters, her baby would inhabit a springtime world.

But the wisdom of old civilizations would be her baby's, too, preserved by her husband's skill in his cooper's trade. Earlier in their voyage, when they were still on the Allegheny River, a crosscurrent had smashed their raft against an island. The twenty-three volumes of the *Encyclopedia Perthensis,* which they had laboriously brought with them from Europe to make their offspring wise, fell into the river. But so watertight was the packing case her husband had fashioned that, with the books as ballast, it bobbed gaily downstream, to be caught by an Indian who was glad to sell it back, white man's knowledge and all, for ten dollars.

Just over the Pennsylvania line, the Blythes put their possessions ashore near East Liverpool, Ohio. While her husband searched the partly settled area for the best piece of unpre-empted forest, Susan Blythe gave birth, on May 9, 1815, to the weeping bundle that was to grow into one of America's most strangely inspired painters.

David Gilmour Blythe was raised in a log cabin. His compulsion to draw caricatures of the neighbors on every available surface—a fragment of slate, the back-house door—indicated to loving eyes a skill with his hands encouraging for a craftsman's son. But certainly there were also less favorable omens: uncontrollable tantrums, inexplicable depressions, unconquerable fears.

At the age of sixteen, Blythe was apprenticed to a wood carver at Pittsburgh, about forty miles upriver. After three years of whittling emblems and architectural decorations, he set himself up as a house painter. But Blythe was restless; soon he left Pittsburgh and sailed downriver to New Orleans. The snags and the jetties, the wood boats and the rafts, the "darkies" loading and unloading to song—all these sights and sounds brought him no comfort. His soul called for something stranger, more impossible, farther away. He journeyed to New York and joined the Navy. But his ship remained in local and Caribbean waters: he found no El Dorado.

His enlistment finally over, Blythe wandered through eastern Ohio and western Pennsylvania, earning a meager living as a self-taught painter of portraits. From the hard, crabbed, minimal likenesses he made, no one could have guessed that his name would one day rank high in the roster of American artists.

Having for five years inched under what he called "the stranger's cold, blank stare" down a seemingly endless vista of small-town boardinghouses, Blythe in 1846 found himself in yet another, this one forty miles south of Pittsburgh at Uniontown, Pennsylvania. He sat silent, a tall, ungainly, red-headed young man, as the regulars roared at the dinner table over a remembered incident: a local peddler had fallen asleep

TEXT CONTINUED ON PAGE 76
ILLUSTRATIONS CONTINUE ON THE FOLLOWING PAGES

This painting, with the bitter title, Art versus Law, *resulted from Blythe's eviction from his studio for nonpayment of rent. Apparently the pathetic figure standing before the locked door is the artist: David Blythe spared no one, including himself.*

POST OFFICE.

GENERAL DELIVERY.

Blythe

Blythe's mood in the painting Post Office *was unusually jocose as he pictured an absurd jam-up of plump citizens, burrowing urchins, and balloon skirts at a narrow delivery window. But even here he could not resist a touch of casual depravity: witness the young pickpocket (left) and the sullenly precocious dwarf of a newsboy (center) puffing on a stogie.*

HORSELAUGH
AT
HUMANKIND

Blythe's invariably comic subject matter masked an angry and tormented view of life, a contempt for the fancies and foibles of the human race. He might well have agreed with Jonathan Swift's character, Captain Lemuel Gulliver, who found man "the most pernicious race of little odious vermin that nature ever suffered to crawl upon the face of the earth." In Blythe's paintings even the animals mocked people. The scene above, for example, shows a mule rearing back in astonishment at the sight of a ridiculously haughty lady in a hoop skirt—upsetting, in the process, cordwood piled on his cart. Below, in an almost haunted winter landscape, a breakaway horse dumps a sleigh and its passengers in the squalid yard of a country inn, and turns as if to snicker at the sight of his victims sprawling in the dirty snow. Meanwhile barroom bumpkins lounge on the porch and a small boy, pulling his sled, runs to see the sudden wreck.

COLLECTION OF MRS. SCREVEN LORILLARD

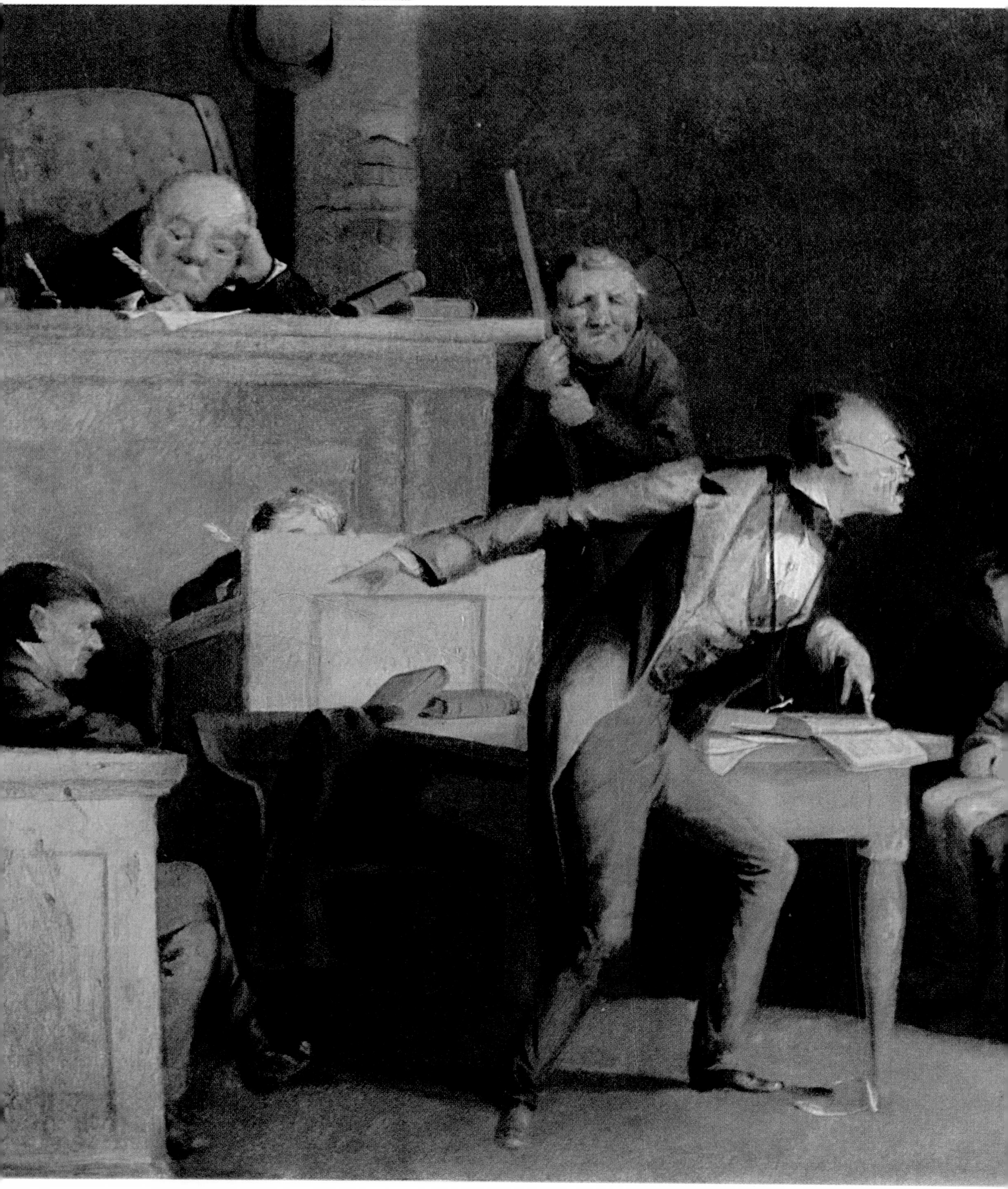

In the Court of His Peers

Courtroom Scene *is the title of this painting, surely one of the Pittsburgh artist's angriest works. As a ranting, demonic prosecutor points a bony finger at a meek and utterly resigned defendant, the attention of the judge wanders, and a jury of slack-jawed rabble can hardly stay awake. It is more than a mere indictment of shoddy procedures in the courts of his time, for Blythe seemed here to be rendering a judgment on man himself. The verdict, which was a foregone conclusion, was Guilty.*

The everyday agonies of life intrigued Blythe. At left above, a man grimaces as he struggles with a boot. In another vignette (right), a schoolboy lights a firecracker with a cigar—youth was always a symbol of malicious mischief.

Blythe's work can be compared to that of William Hogarth, and in their treatment of the coarse life of the street, the market, and the tavern there is more than a passing similarity. Certainly the painting above, Pittsburgh Horse Market, *with its spavined, half-starved, and mistreated nags (who can still muster the spirit to bite back at their human tormenters), its grotesque hagglers, and its malevolent ruffian of an auctioneer (wielding a whip, center), is a conception worthy of the great English satirist. At right is another example of Blythe's varied talent, an eight-foot-high carved wood statue of Lafayette, still standing at the Fayette County Courthouse in Uniontown, Pennsylvania.*

A PITTSBURGH HOGARTH

In his last years, Blythe was fascinated by Civil War subjects. Above, Union troops entrain for camp. The 1862 painting below shows Lincoln, fettered by the obstructionist Democrats of Tammany Hall, striking the dragon, the Confederacy, with a gun swab.

Among the many treasures left behind by that highly literate Chief Executive, Woodrow Wilson, is a storehouse of 1,400 letters between him and his first wife, Ellen Axson Wilson, whom he married in 1885 and who died in the White House in 1914, during his first term.

It is something of a historical event that a representative selection from these letters is now to be published, skillfully edited in a book entitled The Priceless Gift, by Mrs. Eleanor Wilson McAdoo, youngest daughter of Woodrow and Ellen Wilson. It offers a matchless and sometimes surprising insight into the character of one of our most famous Presidents. In the letters to the girl he loved, Wilson exposed his deepest feelings without concealment or restraint. Many of his well-known traits—idealism, intensity, uncompromising integrity, persistence—are amply seen; but unfamiliar facets are also revealed—drollery, self-mockery, even jealousy.

The Priceless Gift will be published later this month by the McGraw-Hill Book Company, and AMERICAN HERITAGE here presents a condensation from the first part of it, covering the courtship of Ellen Axson and Woodrow Wilson, from their meeting in 1883 until their marriage in 1885. Not only do these letters tell us very much about the remarkable couple who wrote them, but they also bring back nostalgically an era when courtship was more decorous, more formal, almost comically elaborate, and yet in some sense more passionate than it is in our times.

Ellen Axson Wilson, 1860–1914

The
COURTSHIP
of
WOODROW
WILSON

By ELEANOR WILSON McADOO

Woodrow Wilson, 1856–1924

There is a city in Georgia called Rome because it is built on seven hills. In 1883 it was a very small city. Gardens enclosed its stately old houses, tall trees sheltered the streets, and no one was ever in a hurry.

On an April Sunday the hills were bright with new grass, and the apple orchards in the valleys were in full bloom. It was a warm day, made for picnics or for lazy talk on cool verandas, but it never occurred to young Thomas Woodrow Wilson to do anything of the sort. All his life, wherever he was, or whatever the weather, he went to church on Sunday.

Wilson was—rather unsuccessfully—practicing law in Atlanta in 1883 and had gone to Rome to consult his uncle, James Bones, about a legal matter. He was twenty-six—a tall, thin young man with large gray eyes, brown hair, side whiskers, and a stubborn chin; a determined young man, with a goal in life. He intended to have a distinguished career. In politics? In the literary world? That remained to be seen. In the meantime, he had discarded his first name. Short, alliterative, and unusual, Woodrow Wilson would be a name not easily forgotten.

Mr. and Mrs. James Bones and their married daughter, Jessie Brower, took Woodrow to their own church, the First Presbyterian, that morning, and his usual Sunday mood of contentment was increased by the fact that his father's friend Mr. Axson was the minister of the church and a very good preacher. Then a girl in a pew near the pulpit turned her head to whisper to the small boy beside her, and Woodrow's attention wandered. Her profile, silhouetted against the black veil draped over her hat, was delightful. A tiptilted little nose, a perfect complexion, a sweetly curved mouth, and hair like burnished copper. Woodrow stared shamelessly until the girl looked again at the preacher; then he forced his eyes and his mind back to Mr. Axson and the sermon. But when the service was over he asked his aunt who the pretty girl was.

"Why, that's Ellie Lou Axson," she told him. She was a "talented artist" and had read "all the classics." She was "one of the rarest and most beautiful girls that ever lived in Rome." Her mother had died in childbirth, and Ellie Lou kept house for her father.

Woodrow decided then and there that it was his duty to call on his father's friend, Mr. Axson, as soon as possible.

Six months later, in a letter to Ellen Louise Axson, he wrote of that first visit,

. . . But though I was still delighted with [your] face, I still at the end of that call could regard it with dispassionate criticism. But . . . it was not very long after that that I walked home with you from Jessie's . . . and I remember leaving you that afternoon with a feeling that I had found a new and altogether delightful sort of companion. Passion was beginning to enter into the criticism, and had pretty nearly gotten the better of it by the time we had climbed to the top of the hill. . . .

Woodrow went back, reluctantly, to the frustrating practice of law in Atlanta. He had about reached the conclusion that he had chosen the wrong profession. Aside from his failure to meet expenses, he did not like the practice of law. He had time and to spare for writing, but not the right environment. The libraries in Atlanta were inadequate, and he had found no intellectual companions. He wrote, finally, to his most valued confidant and friend, his father, and asked for advice. The Reverend Joseph Wilson suggested that he give up his law practice and take a postgraduate course at Johns Hopkins University. After that he could easily earn a living as a professor and a writer.

A few weeks before, Woodrow would have readily agreed to this plan, but ever since he had left Rome he had been haunted by a pair of luminous brown eyes and tormented by the thought that he had not made a good impression on Miss Ellie Lou Axson. He knew now that he was in love with her, and he was afraid that if he went to Johns Hopkins he would lose her. He knew one thing for certain. He must see her again —soon—and try to find the courage to tell her that he loved her. If she returned his love, he would try to overcome his distaste of the law and make a success of it. In June, like an answer to prayer, Uncle James Bones asked him to come again to Rome for further consultation.

A few days later, in a hired buggy, Woodrow drove Ellen through the apple orchards of the countryside near Rome, doing his best to be impressive but not impetuous. Ellen was very shy, Woodrow painfully self-conscious. She had very little to say. He talked too much. But after he had left her at the parsonage, he comforted himself: she had listened closely to everything he said, and agreed with most of it.

Uncle James Bones, briefed by his daughter on the budding romance, deliberately prolonged his consultations with his nephew. So Woodrow stayed on for a week or more and saw Ellen as often as possible. He called on her, escorted her to prayer meeting, took her to a concert, and monopolized her at picnics arranged by Jessie Brower. Again and again he tried to tell her that he loved her, but kept putting it off, waiting for some sign that she cared for him. Then, one day, there was a sign. Jessie had planned another picnic, and in reply to Woodrow's invitation, Ellen wrote:

Mr. Woodrow,
Very unwillingly and with the firm conviction that I am the

most unfortunate of mortals, I write to tell Jessie that I won't be able to go on the picnic. . . . I last evening made an ill-timed engagement to take a boat-ride on that afternoon and, like Sterne's starling, "I can't get out of it." . . .

There is no reason, not even—strange to say—any *disinclination*, to prevent my saying most truthfully that I will be happy to walk with you this afternoon. With love to Jessie, I remain,

Your sincere friend,
Ellen L. Axson

He read it again. For a very reserved young lady it was a breath-taking note. And she had called him "Mr. Woodrow"! The probability that this was due to absent-mindedness was significant. He was Woodrow now in her secret thoughts. He decided that, during their walk, it would be safe to at least hint that he was in love with her. He wrote later:

. . . I remember walking one afternoon in the early summer with a certain sweet friend of mine. We had chosen the railroad bed because it led along the bank of the river and

ber, he went to Asheville, North Carolina, at his father's request, to take care of some matters connected with Dr. Wilson's work with the Southern Presbyterian Assembly. And there, standing at the window of his hotel room, he saw the figure of Miss Ellie Lou Axson vanishing down the street. He had not known that she was in Asheville, and he might have failed to recognize her if it had not been for one small detail—the way she coiled her hair at the back of her head. Woodrow Wilson got to the street in a matter of seconds, caught up with Ellen, found out where the friends she was visiting lived, and begged her to see him very soon.

There followed three enchanted days. On the last afternoon, too desperately in love to remember his uncertain future, Woodrow proposed, and Ellen, immediately and joyfully, said "Yes."

He could hardly believe it. Weeks later he wrote,

My precious Ellie,
Sometimes when I think of our engagement I wonder if I have not been dreaming the last two months. When I recall

How can a fellow in Baltimore write a lecture on Adam

would lead us to where we would find a seat near the water on a big jutting rock which stood with its feet in the river commanding a view of one of the prettiest bends of the stream. Not an incident of that walk have I forgotten . . . I was quite conscious that I was very much in love with my companion and I was desperately intent upon finding out what my chances were of winning her.

Nothing conclusive happened, although, as Woodrow wrote Ellen afterward, he thought she must be aware of his feelings.

. . . You knew that I loved you before I told you, didn't you, love? Why, I had told you often enough by plain enough signs, and even by pretty plain words. Do you remember the verses I gave you as we rode home from a picnic? I remember the charming blush with which you read them, but did not dare interpret it as I wished I might. Did you imagine that I had copied all those lines to give you just because I thought them pretty and hoped they would interest you from a literary point of view? . . .

Their next meeting was not planned. Ellen and Woodrow were always sure that it was arranged by the kind Providence in which they both believed. When the firm of Renick and Wilson finally gave up the struggle to make ends meet, Woodrow decided to go to Johns Hopkins for one year, although he was not happy about the financial sacrifice his parents would have to make. Before going to Baltimore, in Septem-

my first feelings for you; how passionate love grew rapidly upon me; how all my thoughts used to center in plans to win you; what castles my hopes used to build and how I used to sicken at the prospect of hope deferred; and then how, much sooner than I had dared to hope, how by a seeming accident, we met and you gave your heart to me, it all seems so like a sweet dream that I am afraid to credit my memory. The impression is perhaps heightened by the fact that I left you before I had time to realize that you had pledged yourself to me. Although you had spoken the words which will always live in my memory, "I will do anything to make you happy"; although I had taken that sweet sealing kiss; and had been permitted to hold you in my arms, I remember calling you "Miss Ellie" to the last and being utterly unable to speak any part of the love and joy that were in my heart. . . .

Sitting dazed and incredulous in the train after he had left her, Woodrow Wilson thought that if she had really accepted him, no success that he might achieve would ever compare with such a victory. He was to believe this all his life. Yet his elation was tempered by a sort of desperation when he faced the fact that he could not ask her to marry him for at least a year—a year at Johns Hopkins, and after that the search for a professorship with sufficient income to support them. Baltimore seemed a bleak and dreary place when he arrived, and the college buildings looked more like a prison than a university when he went to register.

The first days were difficult. He spent most of them looking for an inexpensive place to live, writing to Ellen, and haunting the post office in the hope of finding a letter from her. No letter came. His parents were vacationing at Arden Park, not far from Asheville. He had asked Ellen to call on them before she went back to Rome. Had something gone wrong there? Had she changed her mind about marrying him? He was frantic.

Balto., Md., Sept. 25th, 1883

My own darling,

I am sick at heart from not hearing from you. It is now a week since you must have reached home and not a line have I had from you. I am filled with apprehensions . . . I know that there must be some reason, but what can it be? . . . The past week has seemed like a month—I am astonished to find that it is still September . . . I found a ring today that suits me and shall send it to you at once . . . I know that you will think it pretty. I have had nothing engraved in it. I preferred having that done after conferring with you and ascertaining your taste and preference in the

Ellen's next letter was written before she received his, and again "observed the laws of climax."

Rome, September 25th, 1883

My dear Friend:

As I find myself today at the most comfortable stage of convalescence, doomed to do nothing at all but enjoy myself, it occurs to me that there is no reason why I should not write a few lines to you, notwithstanding my long scrawl of yesterday. . . .

I thank you very much for sending your dear mother's note and *with all my heart* I thank her and your father for their kind words. . . . In truth, I was frightened beyond measure—no, not frightened exactly; yet that word must answer for lack of better. I can usually exercise a fair amount of self-control, provided always I am not taken unaware . . . But as we drove through Arden Park, I certainly felt it oozing out of the tips of my fingers; as I took off my hat I could see for myself that I was positively *pale* with fright —or whatever it was—and I couldn't for the world have told then why or wherefore.

Smith when he's forever thinking of a girl in Georgia?

matter. I want you to wear the ring as it is until I can come to you. Then we can have what you please put in it and I can put it on your hand with appropriate ceremonies of our own invention, and of which I should like to have the direction!

With a heart brimful of love
Your own
Woodrow

Two days later Ellen's first letter came, explaining why she had not written sooner. She had returned from Asheville to find her father quite ill and her younger brother, Edward, with a fever. They now needed all of her time and love to cure them. Woodrow wrote at once,

Balto., Md., Sept. 27th, 1883

My own darling,

. . . I cannot describe to you my delight at the receipt of your letter. I had come away from the postoffice with a heavy heart so often that the revulsion of feeling was tremendous when I took your letter from the envelope and I was almost frightened at the way my heart beat. It was the sweetest letter ever written—and it seems to have been written with great rhetorical art for it observed the laws of climax, beginning "My dear Friend" (as if I were nothing more!) and ending with confessions of love which are the sweetest, as well as the most modest that ever a maiden made. . . .

. . . I have scarcely left myself light or space to say once again that *I love you.* Ah, my darling, I have no words—will never find them—to tell you how much; nor how very happy it makes me to hear you say—and repeat it—that you love me. Whenever I read it in your letters, were it several times on one page, it gives me a new and distinct thrill of delight. Goodnight, dear love.

Yours with all my heart,
Ellie

Now that Woodrow was settled and happy in the sure knowledge of Ellen's love, he was able to concentrate on his work. Every day except Sunday was taken up with classes and long hours of study, yet he never failed to write to Ellen two or three times a week and to read her letters over and over. It was difficult for her, brought up to conduct herself with extreme reserve and modesty, to write a love letter. Woodrow was also reserved, to a fault, but he had no inhibitions where his beloved was concerned. He opened his mind and soul to her, as well as his heart, and, pleading, teasing, and praising by turns, tried to persuade her to follow his example.

Balto., Md., Sept. 29th, 1883

. . . Your sweet letters . . . fill me with indescribable delight: all the more because I know that such confessions cost you a little struggle with your natural shyness in such matters. I love you with all my heart, my darling, and it makes

CONTINUED ON PAGE 67

Petersburg and the Mine

As this section of the diary opens, the Army of the Potomac has just arrived in front of Petersburg, Virginia, a railroad junction point whose capture would compel the Confederates to evacuate Richmond. Grant's forces reached Petersburg before most of Lee's army did, but the opening attacks were bungled and the armies settled down to siege warfare much like that which characterized the trenches in France in World War I. Grant's one chance for a break-through came late in July, when the explosion of a mine opened a gap in the Confederate lines.

IN FRONT OF PETERSBURG, JUNE 17, FRIDAY We travelled very slowly, with constant stops and then a few yards gained. Take it altogether, I do not remember ever to have seen such an amount of sleepiness on the part of both officers and men. About two o'clock in the morning, finding the provost guard and those immediately in their front hauled off the road and lying down, I took it for a general halt. All my staff were soon asleep too on the roadside: I tried it myself, but, though my eyelids ached from sleepiness, I could not lose myself even for a moment.

We had probably been here for an hour or more when an aide came up and told me the corps was in camp about a mile on. We at once now pushed on; I saw the general, got my orders from him, as sleepy as myself, parked my batteries, gave my own orders, and was asleep *in bed* as quick as it could be done. About eight o'clock I was awakened with orders to have my command in readiness to move at very short notice. I rode up to Warren's quarters, and afterward with him to the front. There had been a good deal of fighting going on all the morning by the Second and Ninth Corps; the former was off to the right, the latter reached to our front. Burnside's negroes, I hear, carried one work, capturing four guns and some prisoners.

AVERY HOUSE, JUNE 18, SATURDAY We might say that we slept under fire last night, for odd shots were constantly coming over our way. So soon as it was light, we found that the enemy had abandoned the rest of this line of works to our left around the Avery house with their main force, leaving only a strong skirmish line, which fell back fighting as we advanced. Lee was putting up an inner line of works, and not having them finished this morning, fought us pretty stiffly all the way back. His batteries were within the new line, but he had a double skirmish line out, and strong bodies of infantry in all the bit of wood we had to pass through.

At three the attack was made, Hart and Bigelow shoving their guns up by hand directly behind the troops, and opening immediately. The fire along the whole line was tremendous on both sides, the battle being in many instances within long canister range of each other. I cannot say that our men went in well, or at all as if they meant to carry the works. In five minutes they were coming back. Finding several hundred men of the fourth division who had come back behind the ridge on which the batteries were, I rode down there, and tried to get them forward again.

Very foolishly, I cried out that I would lead them myself; and in the excitement of the moment I should have done it on horseback I believe, had the men gone, but not over some two dozen would budge. Had they gone I should probably have made no more entries here. In some fifteen or twenty minutes the whole attack had proved a failure, though it was some time longer before all our men got back out of the valley.

All the batteries of my brigade have been engaged throughout the day, firing a total of near 4,000 rounds. During the attack I was on top of the knoll where Hart and Bigelow were, mounted, until our men began to fall back. A piece of a laid-up shell passed through my pants and drawers directly under the right knee, cutting as square at its entrance as if done by a pair of scissors.

How it went where it did I cannot see, the holes looking as if the shot must have gone directly through the leg.

JUNE 19, SUNDAY This has been a day of rest; that is, so far as remaining under a constant fire of musketry, and an occasional outpouring of artillery can be called rest. As to getting the men up to assaulting point, I do not believe it possible; never has the Army of the Potomac been so demoralized as at this time.

General Hunt was here today and visited all our line. When we went out to Bigelow's battery we found it very hot; the bullets from the rebel line whizzed about our ears at the rate of at least thirty a minute. I do not remember ever being more scared, and we crept up to the guns almost on our hands and knees. Yet this is the same ground on which two days ago I rode about mounted, when there was a hundred times as much firing. Could there be a stronger proof that courage is merely a non-realization of the danger one is in owing to excitement, responsibility, or something of the sort?

JUNE 24, FRIDAY The weather has been waxing warmer the last two days, and today has been really a piper. Fortunately I have next to nothing to do, but try to keep cool and kill time. The men in the trenches, though, must suffer very much from this great heat.

Maj. Gen. G. K. Warren, head of the Fifth Corps; in Leslie's, Aug. 13, 1864.

Everything remains stationary in front of Petersburg. I see no prospect of our being any more expeditious in reducing this place than McClellan was, in front of Yorktown. We have already lost three or four times as many men as he did there, and have done nearly if not quite as much digging. Yet operations have not begun here; it is neither a siege nor an investment as yet, nor do I hear of anything being determined on. I fear that the truth is that all the fight is gone out of our men. Grant has used the army up, and will now have to wait until its morale is restored before he can do anything.

JUNE 30, THURSDAY   I have said nothing about War Department orders this month, having enough else to fill up; nor as to Banks's incompetency on the Red River. In looking over the orders I find nothing of moment, save one in which the President commutes the death punishment of all deserters to imprisonment during the war. Poor, weak, well meaning Lincoln!

JULY 7, THURSDAY   The Fourth of July passed without any very great observance by the Army. Having some of my Christmas box still on hand, we made quite a spread for us. The "pièce de résistance" was salmon and green peas, both of which were canned somewhere in France at least a year ago. Still, they were as fine and delicate as when first put up; quite equal to any I have ever eaten. 'Tis singular that our people cannot learn to can these things as well as the French; or rather it would be were not the French the best cooks in the world, while the Americans are the worst. Our sutler brought us some champagne, but it was of the poorest Jersey brand. I could not drink a glass of it myself.

Speaking of drinks, General Burnside would appear to like them as well as his staff. I was over there one day to call on some of them, when happening to enter his camp near the general's tent, I found him sitting in front of it in his shirt sleeves, alongside of a great pile of boxes labelled ale, cider, and whiskey. The general insisted on my taking some, so I drank a pint of cider with ice, which was most excellent.

JULY 10, SUNDAY   Siege operations here have been at last determined on; the order, which I have not yet seen, was issued yesterday. I only know that the approaches are to be made from the front of this corps and the Ninth.

We are still without rain, and as there has been so much turning up of the dirt, the slightest wind renders the dust intolerable. It fills our tents even here at headquarters, where there is but little passing close by, making everything very dirty.

JULY 17, SUNDAY   Dry, dry, dry; the leaves are as brass so far as their giving any moisture goes. The dust is intolerable; such as can only be equalled in the Sahara during a simoon. It has got so driven into the dark blue of our men's coats that even the neatest of them look shabby. The great heat, however, has passed, but left its mark in a large increase of fever patients in our hospitals.

They say that Burnside is tunneling for a mine somewhere, but I have heard nothing particular about it as yet.

JULY 19, TUESDAY   The news of the day, most welcome too, is the arrival of rain. Even in the midst of a siege, those things which add most to one's comfort hold the first place in interest.

JULY 21, THURSDAY   We are having cool weather after our rain; the nights really cold with their heavy dew. The dust, too, is already beginning to get up again. Work still goes on steadily.

The mine which General Burnside is making causes a good deal of talk and is generally much laughed at. It is an affair of his own entirely, and has nothing to do with the regular siege operations, or the engineers with it. The rebels somehow, probably from deserters, have got information of it, and the men there seem to laugh at it too, as their pickets are constantly asking after its welfare. I know nothing about it myself save that it is somewhere opposite the Taylor house, where Burnside's lines come up very close to those of the enemy. Our engineers say that it is badly located. Neither they, Meade, nor the other corps commanders have any belief in its success.

JULY 24, SUNDAY   Certain changes in the plan of operations here were decided on Friday night which will tend to hurry up the first scene in the tragedy. It was determined to adopt Burnside's mine, which has been successfully made, and try that way of getting into the rebel lines.

Yesterday I spent the whole day with Hunt and Duane on our line, deciding where artillery to cover the assault was to be placed. Two batteries for four guns each are to be added between Ayres and Fort Hell; the works on the right, which are miserably planned, are to be rebuilt, and two large mortar batteries are to be erected for ten and eight-inch pieces.

JULY 28, THURSDAY   The works preparatory to the explosion of the mine are progressing rapidly. I have been all along our line with General Hunt today, making the final arrangements as to the placing of the guns. Saturday is now fixed on as the day of assault. The present plan is for twelve guns on the extreme right, twelve more where Ayres's batteries are, ten in two works between there and Fort Hell, and eight in that work; six of them siege guns. I have not yet quite decided on what batteries to place in each position; but have six batteries of the Sixth Corps placed at my disposal.

Mortar practice has got to be quite the fashion on both sides. I have not allowed any of the pieces on our front to be fired since I regained control of them, except when the enemy persevered in firing. But Burnside has blazed away pretty freely, all his artillery being subject to the division commanders.

JULY 29, FRIDAY   Had a hard day's work today, not getting to bed until half-past one at night. All my guns

The Plot That Failed

The Battle of the Crater, which followed the explosion of a huge mine under a Confederate strongpoint on July 30, 1864, was one of the dramatic incidents of the siege of Petersburg, as described in Colonel Wainwright's diary. Some of its tense moments are depicted in the contemporary sketches on these pages. Upper left: an artist for Leslie's *drew Lieutenant Colonel Henry Pleasants supervising the mining operation; right: A. R. Waud of* Harper's Weekly *sketched Union soldiers carrying powder to the mine entrance and (far right) Colonel Pleasants directing the placing of the powder kegs in the mine itself. The large sketch below, drawn by Andrew McCallum for* The Soldier in Our Civil War, *reconstructs the actual explosion of the charge. The Federal artillery, shown in the foreground firing on the Confederate line, actually opened fire (as Colonel Wainwright makes clear) after the blast, to pave the way for an infantry charge—which failed miserably.*

Petersburg Railroad   Confederate Fort.   Confederate Mortar Battery.   City of Petersburg.

BEFORE PETERSBURG, JULY 30TH, 1864. — EXPLOSION OF THE MINE, A

Ninth Corps Battery.   Explosion of the Mine.

ARGE ON THE CONFEDERATE WORKS.—From a Sketch by Andrew McCallum.

are in position and the officers have full and particular instructions, so that knowing my men I have every confidence that the artillery part of the affair tomorrow on this front will be well done.

So soon as it became quite dark, we began moving guns into position. It was a most favorable night, just light enough to see our own way about, without enough for the enemy to discern our movements; with a gentle breeze blowing directly from them. By midnight I had seen every gun in its place, and instructed, questioned and cross-questioned all my commanders; each one of whom I had taken to his position during the day and pointed out to him exactly what he was to do.

JULY 30, SATURDAY   The mine has exploded but we are not in Petersburg. The affair proved a fiasco, a most miserable fizzle. Never before have I felt that the Army of the Potomac was disgraced; failed it has frequently, and botches its commanding generals have made of more than one piece of work, but the army itself has always come out with honour. The only comfort I have tonight is that the artillery part of the business was *perfect*.

But to particulars, and first as to the ground. The rebel lines in this part are tolerably near straight, running north and south from the foot of Cemetery Hill to the great salient. Behind them the ground rises in a gentle slope to considerable height; along the top of which, and parallel to their works, is the Jerusalem Plank Road. I should say it might be an average of three or four hundred yards between the lines and the road. All this ground is open, without wood save detached trees, until you get near the cemetery, where there is a small copse in a little ravine. The battery under which the mine was placed was about a hundred and fifty yards in front and to their right of this copse.

At three o'clock we were all up. Day was hardly dawning; breakfast did not take long. I planted my flag where I had indicated that headquarters would be during the affair, immediately in rear of the great mortar battery. From a mound of dirt here I could see the whole rebel line from Cemetery Hill south, and all my own batteries from Fitzhugh to Phillips.

When I reached my post our lines were all alive. No fires had been allowed, but the men had made a cold breakfast and were ready for work; every piece was loaded and pointed, while the officers of each battery could be seen looking earnestly for the signal.

Half-past three, the hour fixed, passed with no explosion. The match had gone out, but Lieutenant-Colonel Pleasants went up the gallery and lit it again. This caused so much of a delay that it was a quarter past four when it went off.

Not sixty seconds elapsed from the moment the doomed work rose in the air before every one of our batteries opened. It was a grand and most impressive sight and sound; in some respects the finest I have seen. The roar was not greater if equal to that at Gettysburg, but there was more variety of notes in it from the number of siege guns and mortars here. Very quickly the whole of our front was covered with a dense cloud of white smoke, so that all objects were obscured from my view save a dim view of the men handling their immense ten-inch shells immediately at my feet, and the rise of a great black ball, with a fiery tail, rolling over and over high up into the air until it was lost in the smoke.

To my view the explosion itself presented nothing but a column of black and white smoke rising perhaps a hundred yards into the air. I presume the guns of the battery and most of the men in it were carried up too, but they were so enveloped in the smoke and dust that I at least could not see them. Our fire was splendid. It was not ten minutes, I think, before the enemy were completely silenced; then I was delighted with the promptness with which nearly all my batteries slackened off their fire to one in which they could take deliberate aim, and watch the course of each shot. The infantry, too, ceased after a time, and I was again able to see something of what was going on. All I could make out was that our men were in possession of the mined battery, as I could discern a number of flags there.

I looked in vain, however, for the prompt movement along the inside of their lines, to right and left; nor was any such move made at any time during the day, or so far as I can learn even attempted. Another thing I noticed, which struck me at the time: I could not see any large bodies of troops passing from our lines across into the rebel works, but a continuous stream of single men or little squads.

So completely did we subdue the enemy fire from their line of works that after the first spurt, they did not throw over a score of shells into our lines. They, however, at times opened briskly from the two batteries on the crest, and from one in the redoubt, on the mass of our men in the crater of the mine; especially after ten o'clock.

My loss today has been almost nothing. Nor can the loss of the infantry in this corps amount to anything much. In Burnside's, I fear, though, it has been heavy. It always is in badly managed affairs, and his men were evidently so crowded in the crater that a single shell exploding among them—and I saw three go off at once in their very midst—must have hurt a great many.

Since returning to camp I learn that the brigade, which was to have charged first, would not go, and another had to be substituted, by which much time was lost after the explosion. Where was the "forlorn hope" of volunteers, supported by the picked regiments of the corps?

A third trouble was that after the first charge the men were not moved over in order, but were directed "to make a run for it" and reform their companies after they got over. Consequently all was confusion in the crowded crater; the good men trying to find their own command and the cowards to hide from it. This alone was sufficient to cause a failure, and it is about the most disgracefully unmilitary thing I have heard of. The general officer who gave such an order, or allowed it to be given, ought to be shot.

JULY 31, SUNDAY   All was quiet last night and has been today, though Meade fully expected a counterattack on our left and rear from Lee. Today there has been a truce about the mine for the burial of our dead, and the removal of the remaining wounded. The crater was evacuated soon after dark last night.

I have learned nothing additional today about yesterday's failure, being busy with the month's returns, and getting everything straight once more. Tomorrow I shall try to get up to headquarters and hear what I can there. The President is at City Point today, whither Grant has gone to consult with him. Did he come down to enter Petersburg in triumph, or, hearing of the fizzle, has he come to insist that "the Army of the Potomac shall do something?" I really could not blame his requiring almost anything to wipe out the disgrace of yesterday; but I much doubt his ability to comprehend the greatness of it. Our loss is now estimated at 2,300.

AVERY HOUSE, AUGUST 2, TUESDAY   Everything has continued quiet since the failure of Saturday last. Lee has made no attempt to return the compliment. As is always the case after a failure, the camps are full of rumors of a change in the command of this

Maj. Gen. Ambrose Burnside commanded troops in the assault on the crater: a drawing from Leslie's.

army. Many are inclined to throw the blame of the failure on Meade. I do not myself think that he is free; but cannot see what fault can be laid at this door, which is not equally close to Grant's. The whole planning of the mine was Burnside's; he actually ranks Meade, and indeed was his commander at one time in this very army. Both these circumstances made it delicate to interfere . . . to any extent until Burnside had failed. So soon as this became certain, however, Meade ought to have stepped in and directed everything. So, too, Grant being Meade's commander, and equally present, should have acted when Meade failed to do so. Everyone I have talked to believes that it could have been made a success in spite of Burnside's miscarriage.

From General Hunt I have learned certain facts which account for the whole thing; but make Burnside's capabilities—for I suppose he has more than the average—perfectly inexplicable to me. Hunt considered the silencing of the guns in the enemy's reentrant a matter of the first importance, and to make sure of it had erected a very strong battery of fourteen siege guns behind a small wood near the Taylor house; all of which guns would bear on the battery of the enemy's when the wood was cleared away. To be sure that this was done, he sent a note to Burnside, by Warner, late in the afternoon reminding him of it. Twice again during the night he sent Warner down to see if it was done, and, if not, to remind Burnside of it.

The last time Burnside replied that as the matter of the first importance now was to keep the enemy ignorant of any special movement on our side, he would not cut the trees down until the mine was exploded, when a strong party of axemen should be there, who could get them all down in a few minutes. The consequence was, as might have been expected, that the trees were not cut at all, and this great battery was unable to fire at all in that direction. How easy it would have been for Burnside to send an officer out to listen if the chopping could be heard even so far off as his own lines!—when I know he would not have heard a sound.

But another thing Hunt told me is still more wonderful. Burnside made no arrangement for his column to get out of his own works! Nor did any of his subordinates think of it. The obstructions in front of them at this point had been made as strong as possible on account of their nearness to the enemy; and no arrangements having been made to remove them, the men could not get through without breaking ranks, or march by the flank. Where was the common sense of the division and brigade officers who commanded the assaulting column, that they did not themselves see that such a matter was provided for? Surely such a lot of fools did not deserve to succeed.

Siege Warfare; the Election of 1864

After the failure of the attack at the crater, siege warfare was resumed. Grant made a number of attempts to extend his left around Lee's right flank, without any success except that these maneuvers compelled Lee to make constant extensions of his undermanned line. Meanwhile, Major General Philip Sheridan scored decisive victories in the Shenandoah Valley, giving encouragement to the battle-weary Union troops at Petersburg. The fall dragged on, President Lincoln won re-election—it might be noted that Colonel Wainwright refused to vote for him—and the bloody year of 1864 ended with the armies still fixed in front of Petersburg.

SEPTEMBER 21, WEDNESDAY   Our receipts are now considerably more than our losses, so there is every prospect

As Colonel Wainwright explains, artillery played an important part in the long siege of Petersburg. For Harper's Weekly, *A. R. Waud sketched a New York battery getting in position.*

In World War I the shelter shown here would have been called a dugout; at Petersburg it was known as a "bomb-proof rifle-pit." The drawing is by A. W. Warren for Harper's Weekly.

Negro troops were prominent in the assault of June 15, 1864, which nearly took Petersburg. Artist E. F. Mullen, in The Soldier in Our Civil War, *showed them with captured cannon.*

of the regiment soon being full to the maximum allowed by law, which it has never yet been. The men coming to me are a fine lot generally; farmers' sons and others from northern New York and some from Canada who are attracted by the high bounties. We have not had such men enlisting since the first furor of patriotism.

Grant's visit to the Valley seems to have worked wonders. Since yesterday noon we have been all jubilant over dispatches telling of a really complete victory gained by Sheridan over Early, in which after a pretty hard fight, he appears to have sent him kiting through Winchester and up the Valley. The fight was on Monday, and at three P.M. yesterday Sheridan is reported at Cedar Creek.

SEPTEMBER 25, SUNDAY Sheridan is still doing good work in the valley. On Thursday, he reports after maneuvering all day he attacked Early at four P.M. in his lines, which were strongly posted at Fisher's Hill, carrying everything before him, and capturing sixteen guns. At times I cannot help thinking that these victories are the beginning of the end, the death-blows to the rebellion. Certain it is that either Sheridan has an overwhelming majority of numbers, or the life has gone out of the rebels.

OCTOBER 9, SUNDAY Since we have again settled down politics have once more begun to occupy much of the talk; I know no other way to express it, for it is mere talk. I have received circulars from Governor Seymour containing the law of New York State with regard to soldiers in the field voting. I do not approve of their voting at all; but, if they must, I think the New York plan by which each man's vote will be deposited in his own town the best. Should I vote it will be for McClellan, or rather against Lincoln.

OCTOBER 13, THURSDAY We have been quite quiet here since Sunday; but rumours of an early move are prevalent, some of them even going so far as to prophecy the fall of Richmond before the election. I have no hope of that long desired event being so soon brought about; but fully expect another winter of it on the sacred soil. There are, however, certain indications of the commencement of the end of the rebellion in the character, numbers, and reports of the deserters who come in. Every morning more or less who have crossed the lines the preceding night are marched up to headquarters. Nor are they all of that wretched, ragged class of stragglers and shirks who have come in previously, but a number of real men, soldiers, are mixed in, who say that their cause is played out; that they have no more hopes of success, and give it up.

My own three years were out yesterday! I came very near forgetting it, for so accustomed have we become to it, that three years of war do not seem so much to look back upon as one did at the time of my first anniversary. I have been trying tonight to recall some of the thoughts and feelings which came across me during the first months of my service, but find it almost impossible.

How completely, too, have my ideas of great men changed in the last three years; not but what I still believe in geniuses like Gustavus, Napoleon and a dozen others perhaps, but when you leave these out and come down to the ordinary man called great, the illusion is completely dispelled, and I see how a mere lucky hit or the fortunate combination of circumstances have given most of them their reputations. I say now without hesitation that there is not a great man living in this country; certainly not a great general in either army or anything approaching to it. The objects of the war, also, have completely changed: the real question of the salvation of the Union has been so completely overlaid by the insurance of a continuation in power of the Republican party that it is only by digging deep down that I can find the object for which alone I am fighting.

OCTOBER 16, SUNDAY All continues quiet here. As the time for the Presidential election draws near, politics absorb more and more of the time and thoughts of officers and men. The camps are full of civilians sent down to secure the soldiers' votes for one side or the other. His party being in power at Washington, the friends of Mr. Lincoln of course outnumber their opponents two to one. There will no doubt be a great deal of influence exerted by some officers over the men under their command.

General Crawford is quite a politician, strong on the side of those in power; from his talk one would be led to believe that nothing but certain ruin was in reserve for the country should Mr. Lincoln not be elected. Hunt, on the contrary, is an out-and-out Democrat, beside being a warm personal friend of McClellan. He holds that the reelection of Lincoln will prolong the war another four years, and then result in the breaking up of the Union. I do not believe in the extreme views of either side. The rebellion must cease in another year from mere inanition in my opinion. The two parties are equally corrupt, and equally far from my views in their extreme doctrines; while I believe both of the presidential candidates to be sound, and almost identical in their personal views. Both of them, too, are wanting in nerve. But Mr. Lincoln is much the worse, I believe, in this respect. We know that he is already completely in the hands of the radicals of his party, while there is at least a chance that McClellan, if elected, may not fall into the same snare.

OCTOBER 20, THURSDAY This evening we can think and talk of nothing but another victory gained by Sheridan in the valley. His dispatch is hardly as bombasting as some of his others, though the little word "I" is to be found in almost every line of it. Sheridan was in Winchester at the commencement of the fight, and General Wright in command. The rebels were the attacking party, and completely successful at first, driving our whole force back four miles and capturing twenty pieces of artillery. Their second attack at one P.M. was repulsed and at three P.M., a counter attack made resulting in a complete victory on our part.

OCTOBER 23, SUNDAY From full reports received from Sheridan and the newspaper accounts, it is now evident that his victory is even more complete than it at first appeared to be. He now claims thirty guns captured and sixteen hundred prisoners. Early's army, they say, is entirely broken up.

OCTOBER 26, WEDNESDAY Another move is on foot; we start at daylight tomorrow. Our whole corps is to go, with four days rations on the men and sixty rounds of ammunition. I am to take but ten rifled and twelve smooth-bore guns with us while the remainder hold the closed forts here.

Last night I sent off my proxy to Mr. Gillender to cast my vote for McClellan. I was at last induced to vote from sheer distrust of those in power now, and the belief that any change must be for the better. As to the radical newspaper charges that McClellan would acknowledge secession if elected, they are absurd nonsense. Major Duane has just returned from home, where he saw McClellan a number of times. General Hunt told me yesterday that Duane related to him a conversation he had had with McClellan, in which the general stated that should he be elected, he expected to be very unpopular the first year, as he should use every power possible to close the war at once, should enforce the draft strictly, and listen to no remonstrance until the rebellion was effectually quashed.

I have just now (ten P.M.) got an order to be ready at four A.M. tomorrow instead of at daylight. We are to make another trial at turning Lee's right so as to get possession of the South Side Road.

OCTOBER 28, FRIDAY Back at the old spot again, and nothing accomplished! Nothing save a few hundred more men laid under the sod, and a thousand or two carried off with a ball in their body or minus a leg or arm. Two years ago such a failure would have raised a hornets' nest about the ears of the commanding general, but now the country is accustomed to it, and the whole thing will be glossed over in some way.

OCTOBER 31, MONDAY The newspapers try to make the best of our failure last week, taking their cue from Grant's dispatch to Washington, in which he calls the move a "reconnoissance." This affords a vast deal of amusement in the army, considering there were greater exertions and preparations made for this expedition than any previous one. There must have been near 40,000 men on the trip, but not more than a quarter of them were really in the fight. I was told at army headquarters that the official reports put our entire loss at 1,904.

NOVEMBER 9, WEDNESDAY The newspapers we received today, and telegrams, we know enough of the election yesterday to show that the democratic hopes of a great change in public sentiment has not been realized; at least the change has not become great enough to induce people to swallow the Chicago pill. The result among those troops who cast their vote in the field in this corps was as follows:

	Lincoln	McClellan	Lincoln's Majority
Pennsylvania	2,962	1,642	1,320
Maryland	1,228	44	1,184
Maine	290	74	216
Michigan	363	252	111
Wisconsin	333	67	266
	5,176	2,079	3,097

For my own part, I am delighted that the election is over, and trust that having entire power secured to them now for another term of four years, the Republican party will prove itself more conservative than has been feared.

NOVEMBER 24, THURSDAY   This is "Thanksgiving Day" all over the country. Great preparations were made in New York City to supply all the soldiers with a turkey dinner, and the papers this week have been full of accounts of the cooking and packing. Unfortunately it did not get down in time for distribution this morning, though the *cargoes* arrived at City Point last night. Captain Steele tells me that the proportion to this corps will be 14,000 pounds of turkey, one hundred barrels of apples, with cranberry sauce and pies in like quantity. As the officers are to get some as well as the men, teamsters, hospitals, and all, the above amount will have to be divided among about 24,000, giving rather over a half-a-pound of turkey, one apple, and a bit of pie to each.

DECEMBER 6, TUESDAY   We, that is the Fifth Corps, are to move tomorrow morning at daylight. It is a mere raiding expedition for the purpose of destroying the Weldon Railroad so far south from Stoney Creek as will prevent Lee from drawing any supplies from that direction. General Warren will have command, and in addition to all the infantry of his own corps, he is to have Mott's division of the Second, and Gregg's division of cavalry.

DECEMBER 6, TUESDAY   The batch of brevets for this corps arrived this evening. I get all those which I recommended for officers who are still present with me; also one for myself. That is an official notice of the appointment from Secretary Stanton, the actual commission depending on the confirmation of the appointment by the Senate. I shall therefore wait until I am confirmed before I assume the title, as I should not at all like to have to fall back to colonel after having once signed myself general.

NOTTAWAY RIVER, DECEMBER 7, WEDNESDAY   We have had a lovely day for this the first stage of our march; clear and soft as June, and an excellent road all the way. Gregg led out with one brigade of cavalry and a horse battery; leaving his other brigade to cover the right flank and the rear.

The head of the infantry column reached this place, Freeman's Ford, about two hours before dark. It was ten o'clock before our headquarters wagons crossed, so that supper could be got ready. I was fortunate enough to get a nice steak and a cup of coffee from the engineers soon after dark along with General Warren. I have never eaten a nicer steak in the field, though it was cooked in a frying pan. Soon after I got the batteries over and in camp, I spread my blankets under the trees about fifty yards above the bridge head and went to sleep.

This was one of the romances of camp life: the soft night air; the tall leafless trees under which we bivouacked, and which stretched all along the south side of the river; the wide open plain on the opposite bank; the bridge, lighted up by great pitch-pine fires; the noise of the men, horses and mules—all contributed to make a picture such as one dreams of.

DECEMBER 8, THURSDAY   I do not know how exactly to designate the spot where we camp tonight; it being merely at a house by the roadside. The master of the house is not at home, having gone, so at least his wife told us, some twelve or fifteen miles off to get salt for putting down his winter's supply of bacon. The poor fellow might as well have saved his time and money, for he will find no pigs to slaughter when he gets back, our men having killed and eaten the two large hogs before dark. I arrived here about four o'clock, and the afternoon having come off somewhat cold, I went into the house to warm myself. Everything shows the poverty of the inhabitants, though the house was a large one, and the builder no doubt at that time thought himself pretty well-to-do in the world. Now the white part of the household were evidently all living in one room: the family consisting, beside the absent man, of a poor sickly-looking wife, with a young babe at the breast, two other children, and a sister of the man, who I suspect was the backbone of the whole establishment.

In this room were two large four-poster bedsteads, and it seemed to be the only place where they had a fire, at the time of our arrival, for they were baking some cakes there in a dutch oven. These cakes consisted of nothing but cornmeal and water, with the addition of a small proportion of wheat flour.

All the infantry were at work today destroying the railroad, and the work was pretty effectually done for some twenty miles between the Nottaway and Meherrin Rivers; the ties being all taken up and the rails heated and bent. Beyond this, we could do nothing save destroy a few culverts. Gregg's cavalry pushed on to the Meherrin and tried to burn the bridge there, but did not succeed. DR. BRIGGS', DECEMBER 10, SATURDAY Last night was very hard on the men; it began to snow soon after dark, followed by a fine rain and cold. This morning everything was sheeted with ice; each spray of the trees and blade of grass was completely coated, making the country a most beautiful sight when the sun came out, but the roads terrible for the footmen. There was more drunkenness among the infantry than on our march out, and one of Stewart's men had got royally tight. This was the only case of either drunkenness or straggling I heard of in my own command during the whole raid. He was in charge of the first sergeant, who got him up to his battery and tied him behind one of the guns, where he marched the rest of the day, and was made sober by the aid of a bucket of water thrown over him every once in a while.

The men had behaved so well up to this afternoon that I am doubly sorry to have a long black mark to set against them. Still, if the story told is true, there was great provocation; not enough to justify their acts at all, but somewhat excuse them. It is said that some two or three dead men, stripped, were found by the roadside by our advance, who were supposed to be some of our men who had got very drunk when we went out, and then been murdered by guerrillas. Just north of Suffolk Court House a naked body was found which was recognized as a sergeant in one of the regiments; and while the men were burying it, a negro came up and said that the man who shot the sergeant was in a house which he pointed out, hid away under some cornshucks in the garret. The lieutenant commanding the ex-sergeant's company thereupon took his men, surrounded the house, searched the attic, and found a man hid there as the negro had described. Leaving the man there, he set the house on fire, and burned the man in it. This is the story as told to me; if all true, including the negro's testimony as to the identity of the murderer of the sergeant, one cannot blame his comrades for taking the law into their own hands.

But now comes the worst. The story spread almost instantly through the column, and the sight of the burning house seemed to raise the devil in the men at once. Scores of men left the ranks, and seizing brands from the burning house, fired every building in sight. None escaped, large and small, pigsties and privies, all were burnt, with barely time allowed for the people themselves to get out, saving nothing. The negroes fared no better than the whites. Every soul was turned adrift to find shelter for the night as best they could. For this barbarism there was no real excuse, unless exasperation and the innate depravity of mankind is one. So pitiable a sight as the women and children turned adrift at nightfall, and a most severe winter night too, I never saw before and never want to see again. If this is a raid, deliver me from going on another.

Abraham Lincoln won a large majority of the soldiers' votes in the 1864 election. Joseph Becker, for Leslie's Illustrated, *pictured soldiers voting near Fort Wadsworth, in the Federal lines at Petersburg.*

Northern civilians did their best, in the fall of 1864, to give the boys away from home at Petersburg a bountiful Thanksgiving dinner, and a Leslie's *artist sketched some of them sitting down to enjoy their feast.*

Late in 1864 General Warren led a raid against the Weldon Railroad, an important Confederate supply line. This sketch from Harper's Weekly *shows how heated rails were rendered unfit for further use.*

"And all about were men crying . . ."

On the other side of the siege lines lay the nearly beaten Confederates, for whom Petersburg and Appomattox were a sad climax to four years of gallant effort. Something of their spirit is preserved in the following excerpts from the memoirs of Berry Benson, a young sharpshooter who with his brother, Blackwood, served in General Samuel McGowan's First South Carolina Brigade. Edited by his daughter-in-law, Susan Williams Benson, the memoirs will soon be published by the University of Georgia Press as Berry Benson's Civil War Book.—Ed.

On Sunday, April 2, 1865 . . . we learned that five miles to our left, at the very point held by McGowan's Brigade all winter, the enemy had stormed and carried the defenses of Petersburg. Our corps commander, General A. P. Hill, had been killed. After stubborn resistance, Fort Gregg had fallen. Petersburg and Richmond were being evacuated; the whole army was in retreat. . . .

Pretty soon, the enemy coming in hot pursuit, we began sharpshooting. Making a stand at any favorable point, we fought the advance skirmishers until they would begin to flank us, then hastily retreated to take up another stand. . . .

In the middle of a large cornfield, we overtook [our] three Brigades, heading now for the Appomattox River, with the intention of crossing to its north side to escape our pursuers and join the army retreating from Richmond. We reached the river in the late afternoon, finding one small boat which would carry perhaps four men, as our only means of crossing. . . .

A few men now chose to remain behind, hoping to avail themselves of this means of escape. The rest of us (probably not more than 1,000 to 1,200 men) turned our faces up the stream and in Indian file followed a footpath along its banks, hoping every minute to reach some bridge or ferry. In single file the Brigades stretched out, reaching far up and down the river. At length (about full dark) there was a halt, and the troops collected in a little hollow. We all lay down on the wet leaves in the wood, tired and hungry, and awaited orders.

Hundreds of questions were asked and doubts freely raised of our ever getting out of this scrape. Here we were, 3 Brigades, cut off from the rest of the army, a swollen river in front, and Grant's army pressing on behind! . . .

After trying in vain to learn something of our plans and prospects . . . I called on the Sharpshooters—all who wished—to follow me that I was going to find Lee's army. . . .

I started off with 15 men besides myself, one of them, a young fellow, barefoot. And a hard march we made. . . . At daybreak Monday, April 3rd, we . . . learned from some soldiers that our Brigade was organizing at Goode's Bridge on the Appomattox, and we headed for it. . . .

Next morning, April 4th, we started early. Being now pretty well rested, we made as good time as possible amongst the straggling troops [Longstreet's men] that now thronged the road. . . . Amid this helter-skelter, dejected crowd, we marched in order, with arms at the "right shoulder." As we passed the weary, exhausted groups, they stared in amazement to see our little band of sixteen, still preserving discipline and—still better —cheerfulness. . . . [We] marched in order, as neatly as on drill, keeping step to the song that Reuben Ruff sang in a clear, ringing voice, one of the best voices in our camp. The song was "Jubilo," a negro song first sung by the Yankees, later becoming a favorite amongst the Confederates. Like schoolboys on a holiday, we joined in Ruff's chorus at the top of our lungs, so that the woods and hills along our march fairly rang with shouts of "Jubilo." . . . At Goode's Bridge we found [that] of our whole Battallion of Sharpshooters—three companies— only forty were left, of which we made 16. . . .

From Goode's Bridge on, our march was one of unremitting fatigue, hunger, trouble, and disaster. . . . Every hour brought news of the capture or burning of portions of our wagon train, while wagons, broken down horses, pieces of artillery, stragglers, and all kinds of munitions of war were being abandoned to fall into the hands of our pursuers. . . .

Straggling became the rule rather than the exception. From sheer weakness and lack of sustenance, many a brave man lagged then behind his command who had never lagged before. The 8,000 who drew up before Appomattox were not 8,000 bodies; it was 8,000 *souls* which still dragged along with them their unwilling bodies, whether or no. . . .

April 9, 1865 we reached the neighborhood of Appomattox and came to a halt and were drawn up in line. . . . Then I saw a Federal officer come galloping in carrying aloft a white handkerchief. . . .

Presently the whisper began to pass from mouth to mouth that it was a flag of truce, and that *General Lee* was about to surrender. . . . The idea was simply preposterous and I hooted it. There had been surrenders and there would be surrenders, but Gen. Lee's army surrender? Never!

The firing had all ceased, and we saw Confederate regiments returning from the field of battle. And now the whole army— and a small one it was—gathered together on a low hill over against Appomattox. And along the ridge of hills opposite were stretched the long dark lines of the enemy. They lay directly in our front, blocking our further retreat. We were drawn up in column of regiments, I believe, and ordered to stack arms. And then the rumor grew louder and more assured that we were indeed about to surrender. . . .

I had been in Prison once, and was not going again. I [decided to] make my way out to join Gen. Johnston in North Carolina. . . . I talked with Blackwood. He was ready to follow me anywhere. . . .

Shortly before this I had gone to General McGowan . . . to ask whether we were going to surrender. I had found him in the woods, crying, half dressed, taking off his old dirty uniform, and putting on a newer brighter one used on state occasions. I did not then need his acknowledgment of our miserable fate.

By that time it had got to be well known amongst the men that Lee had determined to surrender, and it was a lamentable spectacle to see how the men took it. Some seemed to be glad that it was all over, but even they, I have no doubt, would have been as ready to charge as the rest, had it been so ordered. But mostly there were sad and gloomy faces. For myself, I cried. I could not help it. And all about were men crying . . .

So Blackwood and I left the little tattered, weary, sad, and weeping army—*our* army—left them there on the hill with their arms stacked in the field, all in rows—never to see it any more. Telling Clarke and Bell goodbye, we crossed the road into the untenanted fields and thickets, and in a little while lost sight of all that told of the presence of what was left of the army that through four long years, time and again, had beaten back its enemy, keeping Richmond, its capital, safe and free. . . .

The Benson boys got as far as Greensboro, North Carolina, only to learn that General Johnston, too, was on the point of surrender. They headed south, arriving in Augusta, Georgia, on May 15, 1865. But by that time, the war was all over.

YELLOW TAVERN, DECEMBER 12, MONDAY Safe back again in our old quarters, without a fight, or any mishap, though we were absent the full six days for which we took supplies. The expedition has been a success, in that it accomplished all it was sent out for, and with small loss.

Fort Stedman and Five Forks

The deadlock at Petersburg continued until late in March, Lee's army constantly growing weaker. On March 25, Lee made a desperate attempt to break Grant's line, attacking a strong point called Fort Stedman. The attack failed, and a few days later Grant took the offensive. General Sheridan, with the cavalry and Major General Gouverneur Warren's Fifth Corps, smashed Lee's extreme right in the controversial battle of Five Forks, during which Sheridan (using authority Grant had given him) removed General Warren from command, turning the corps over to General Charles Griffin. Sheridan's complaint that Warren was late in getting his men into action and that he handled them inefficiently once they did get in has not been generally accepted by military historians, and years later a Court of Inquiry exonerated the luckless Warren. In any case, the fall of Petersburg and the evacuation of Richmond came as a direct result of the victory at Five Forks, and Lee's army began its tragic retreat to Appomattox.

MARCH 26, SUNDAY Yesterday morning the long quiet of the winter was broken at the first streak of dawn by a very decided attack on our lines. It was a well conceived affair, a complete surprise, and successful in its first step. If the rebels had as much fight in them now as they had at Gettysburg, they might possibly have driven us out of this entirely, though I am by no means sure of it, for after their first dash all would have been open country.

I was first awakened by an order from General Hunt to turn out all my batteries, and to send word to General Parke that they were at his service. I was partially dressed in one minute and out of my tent: the sun was not yet up: the roar of artillery was constant and very loud: I believe it was not more than twenty minutes from the time of my getting Hunt's first order until the time the two batteries started.

When, an hour or so later, the firing slacked off I went up to army headquarters to hear exactly what was the matter, as I knew nothing beyond the fact that the enemy had broken through our lines at Fort Stedman. I left everything in camp ready for whatever might turn up.

Fort Stedman is, I believe, the farthest to the right of any of our enclosed works. The attack is said to have been made by two divisions, small ones I judge, and was under General Gordon. Lee's intention doubtless was to seize the high ground, clean out our line to Appomattox and so cut off our communications with City Point. But his troops were evidently not willing, and the reports of deserters, that their men would not attack, proved to be

essentially correct. The time lost by Gordon's reserves not coming up enabled Parke to get a line formed on this ridge, and to garnish it with a number of guns from his left, so that the captured work became too hot for its holders; and when Hartranft's division was thrown forward, they recaptured all our line with little trouble.

The whole army is feeling very jubilant today over the affair, and as General Meade said to me this morning, "wish they would try it every day." What will be the next move a very few days will now show.

WHITE OAK ROAD, APRIL 1, 1865, SATURDAY This has been the most momentous day of the war so far, I think; a glorious day; a day of real victory.

During the morning Sheridan advanced with his cavalry from Dinwiddie Court House, the enemy falling back skirmishing to the White Oak Road, where the Ford Road crosses it, at a place called the Five Forks. Here they had a line of low breastworks thrown up. Warren and the whole of the Fifth Corps [were] to attack along the east flank, swinging around to the west with its pivot on the White Oak Road. Ayres's division held the left, Winthrop's brigade crossing the road diagonally. Crawford was on Ayres's right, and Griffin in rear of Crawford.

When I reached Warren, he was in conversation with General Sheridan, close behind Ayres's second line. Our skirmishers were just engaging, the men beginning to advance and rebel bullets coming over our way.

As our men passed through a narrow belt of woods, I could not see the actual charge on the works, only the smoke of the battle. The cheers of our men, however, told me that all was going well, and long files of prisoners coming in soon showed that the works were carried.

I do not think that it was over twenty minutes from the time I left Warren before I saw the first [column of about 1,000] prisoners. These men all moved along cheerfully, without one particle of that sullenness which formerly characterized them under similar circumstances. They joked with our men along the line and I repeatedly heard them say, "We are coming back into the Union boys, we are coming back into the Union." It was a joyful and an exciting sight, seeming to say that the war was about over.

This procession of prisoners was soon followed by another quite as numerous or even larger.

I then passed out onto the White Oak Road, and rode up it westward as the firing was becoming more distant.

At the Forks I found two guns, three-inch, just in their works, and Pennington sitting on one of them. I stopped here and had a talk with him and several other cavalry officers, formerly light battery commanders. They told me that they had charged the works at this point and carried them with any number of prisoners. While there Crawford came down the Ford Road, from the north, looking for Warren: and told me that there were more guns up the road which his men had taken. I went up the Ford Road then; some fifty yards up I found another gun, unlimbered and pointing east; perhaps a hundred yards further on two more standing in the road limbered. This made a total of *five* three-inch guns.

I turned back and pushed along the White Oak Road to find Warren. It was growing dark, the sun having already set; the bugles were sounding the recall; the pursuit was over, and the divisions getting together for the night. I told the General about the guns, and asked if I was to look after their removal. For this he referred me to Sheridan, as he said there might be some jealousy on the part of the cavalry.

We rode back together looking for Sheridan, and found him with his staff about a fire near the west end of the rebel works. Here I waited while General Warren had a short conversation with Sheridan. I dismounted, reported to Sheridan the number of guns I had found, and asked if he wished me to remove them; at the same time stating that Pennington claimed to have captured at least two of them. Sheridan was very pleasant, said that there was glory enough for all, and wished me to look after the guns.

[I] told Warren what directions Sheridan had given me, and inquired where corps headquarters would be for the night. Warren replied that General Sheridan had just informed him that he had relieved him from the command of the corps, and turned it over to Griffin; that he had given no reason for so doing, but referred him to General Grant to whom he was to report for orders.

I was astonished at this news and could not imagine what the trouble was. [Later I learned] that in swinging around Crawford's division separated from Ayres's, keeping off too much to the north; that Warren sent twice to recall him; and finally went himself and brought the division round. Griffin meantime seeing the gap left between the Second and Third divisions, closed up on Ayres's left and took the place Crawford should have occupied. It was Warren's having to go himself to bring Crawford back which was the immediate occasion of his removal, though it could not have been the actual cause.

To me his removal at this time, and after the victory had been won, appears wrong and very cruel. It seems that even had he been removed just before, the victory should have covered up very big faults, and Sheridan should have restored him at once.

Appomattox Court House

In his retreat from the Petersburg lines, Lee was trying to evade Grant's army and join forces with General Joseph E. Johnston, who had a Confederate army near Raleigh, North Carolina, where he faced a much larger Union army under General William

T. Sherman. Sheridan commanded the Union advance, outdistanced the weary, half-starved Confederates, and brought them to bay at Appomattox Court House, where Lee found his army completely boxed in by a Union force that greatly outnumbered his own. Union artillery saw little action during the pursuit, but Wainwright did reach Appomattox in time to get his guns in line ready for the final battle which was never fought.

NEAR SOUTHERLAND'S STATION, APRIL 2, SUNDAY   No fighting today for the Fifth Corps; only a hard and tiring march. I was still sitting by where our tents had been trying to finish a short letter home, when cheer after cheer rang from the troops along the road. I supposed that Sheridan was riding by; for he excites the greatest enthusiasm among the men, and is greeted whenever seen with such cheers as I have not heard given to any officer since McClellan's day.

But this time I was mistaken—the hurrahs were for the fall of Petersburg this morning, news of which had just arrived.

ON RIVER ROAD NEAR DEEP CREEK, APRIL 3, MONDAY   There was an alarm on Crawford's front during the night, and considerable firing on the part of his men. Some stray body of rebels ran against while trying to join their main force.

I pushed to the front myself and found Sheridan and Griffin at a small house near two miles from where we started from. While at this house, I saw a good deal of Sheridan; he appeared exceedingly affable and pleasant in his intercourse with his staff, but certainly would not impress one by his looks any more than Grant does. He is short, thickset, and common Irish looking. Met in the Bowery, one would certainly set him down as a "b'hoy"; and his dress is in perfect keeping with that character. His Irish blood shone out today in the haphazard way he drove ahead, first on one road, then on another, seeming to think that infantry and artillery could go wherever his own horse did, and a whole corps turn in an equally small space.

We received a dispatch from army headquarters, saying that Richmond was evacuated last night. To all intents the rebellion may be said now to be over; certainly it is on its last legs. If those legs are long enough to enable Lee to get around us and join Johnston in North Carolina, they may be strong enough to give us one more big fight. All the heart and spirit being gone, though, strength of leg is not likely to amount to much.

APPOMATTOX COURT HOUSE, APRIL 9, SUNDAY   I may head the account of this day in large letters for its events close the rebellion. The Army of Northern Virginia under Lee has been its main strength, and today that army has surrendered. During three long and hard fought campaigns it has withstood every effort of the Army of the Potomac: now at the commencement of the fourth, it is obliged to succumb without even one great pitched battle. Could the war have been closed with such a battle as Gettysburg, it would have been more glorious for us; more in accordance with what poetical justice would seem to owe to the Army of the Potomac. As it is, the rebellion has been worn out rather than suppressed. The 9th of April will, however, be a day forever to be remembered with thanksgiving throughout our land.

Sheridan's cavalry struck the head of Lee's retreating army last night near Appomattox Station on the railroad, and was able to seize and hold the road to Lynchburg in advance of them; the main road at this point coming down quite near to the railroad. With the first break of day our Corps was again in motion. On arriving at the station after a couple of hours' march, the corps was massed a short distance to the north of it.

The country here is broken into abrupt hills, but is mostly cleared. I found a superb position for my guns near a house, and just where the right of the Fifth Corps joined the Army of the James.

From here we could look down into a valley stretching to the north for some three miles. Immediately below lay the little village of Appomattox Court House into which our skirmishing line was just driving the enemy. Beyond was one mass of men, wagons and artillery; in the distance they appeared to be in utter confusion. Shells from the right and left were bursting in their midst, especially from the right away off to the north where the Second and Sixth Corps were. Little puffs of smoke, too, showed our skirmish line pushing in from the east, as far as the eye could reach.

I at once ordered Rogers up on the left of the house, leaving Mink below as the range was too great for his guns. Just as the guns were in the act of being unlimbered, a flag of truce came galloping up, when all firing was immediately stopped. Rogers and his men were greatly disappointed in not getting a last shot at the rebellion; for Lee's army presented a perfect target for long-range firing. In about an hour we received orders for a suspension of hostilities until three o'clock to arrange terms of surrender. During this time both armies were to remain exactly as they were.

Soon after three o'clock we received notice that the surrender of the Army of Northern Virginia was agreed on. The notice did not reach Humphreys until a little after the appointed time. The instant time was out, he commenced to advance and his batteries opened a vigorous cannonade. For a few minutes we thought that the fight was opened in earnest; but Meade quickly stopped it. An hour or so before dark, we received a circular announcing the surrender of Lee's Army and directing that we go into camp, make ourselves comfortable and send for rations and supplies.

So ends the great rebel army: *the* army of the rebellion.

For I doubt if the force Johnston has in North Carolina amounts to very much, and it is the only army worth calling such they have left east of the Mississippi. Set aside the cause in which it was engaged, the history of the Army of Northern Virginia has been a glorious one. There cannot, however, be much of it left in the valley below tonight, for since this campaign opened by the attack on Fort Stedman, we must have taken near 30,000 prisoners, while very larger numbers have no doubt deserted since they left Richmond and Petersburg, seeking to reach their homes across the country.

APRIL 10, MONDAY   I rode in to look at the rebel camp today, but found that the lines were not yet open for general passing. I was, however, far more fortunate than I expected, for I chanced to get down to the lines while Grant and Lee were having their last interview, which gave me an excellent opportunity to see the latter. Lee is a fine, English looking man; somewhat stout, with a florid complexion and white hair; his appearance is decidedly that of a gentleman. The meeting took place near a small stream, in the road, and all were mounted. What its object was, or what was said on either side, I do not know. In the Tavern, I saw Longstreet, Pickett, Gordon, Heath, and a number of their other generals. The grey uniform is very handsome when good, and new; setting off a fine looking man to great advantage.

Tonight the men are celebrating the surrender with improvised fireworks. It was some time before I could make out how they managed to obtain what appeared to be hundreds of roman candles, but at last discovered that they were shooting rebel fuses from their muskets with small charges of powder. These exactly resembled the balls thrown out by roman candles. The effect together with the camp fires, was really beautiful.

The last act . . . General Robert E. Lee returning to his beaten army after the surrender at Appomattox Court House. Colonel Wainwright tells about the event, depicted here by the artist W. L. Sheppard.

Above the rush of wind and water could be heard their hymns of praise as they sprang from the shallop onto the rock, the stern-faced men in wide-brimmed pot hats, the women modestly poised between this world and the next. So the landing of the Pilgrim Fathers at Plymouth seemed to generations of American schoolchildren nurtured on Felicia Hemans' poem with its later visual embodiments in the paintings of Henry Sargent and Peter F. Rothermel. Even after World War I, when I attended the Tileston School in Mattapan, a small suburb of Boston, a steel engraving of Rothermel's *Landing of the Pilgrims* still hung in the assembly hall. The men wore full-dress Pilgrim uniforms with flowing black capes; the women decorously kept their trailing voluminous skirts under control despite the near-tempest. Their eyes either rolled toward heaven or glanced meekly down at Mother Earth. Never did they stare at the profane space between. As soon as they stepped ashore they knelt in prayer, within a few feet of the landing rock, indifferent to any seventh wave. This upward fixation of the eyes gave a walruslike aspect to many of the males, particularly the bald elders. But at the Tileston School we never doubted the accuracy of the portrait.

In Miss Kelley's fifth grade we still memorized Mrs. Hemans' poem, declaiming separately and then in unison:

> *The breaking waves dashed high*
> *   On a stern and rock-bound coast,*
> *And the woods, against a stormy sky,*
> *   Their giant branches toss'd;*
>
> *And the heavy night hung dark*
> *   The hills and waters o'er,*
> *When a band of exiles moor'd their bark*
> *   On the wild New England shore....*
>
> *Aye, call it holy ground,*
> *   The soil where first they trod!*
> *They have left unstain'd what there they found—*
> *   Freedom to worship God!*

I wondered a little about the "stern and rock-bound coast," for Plymouth was only forty miles away, and I knew that the shore there was flat and sandy. But that the

Peter F. Rothermel's Pilgrims, in this 1869 engraving, seem concerned less

Mayflower was not a bark, that the "soil where first they trod" was really where fourth they trod, were facts much too esoteric to have reached us. Mrs. Hemans' insistent imagery became lodged permanently in our minds. Whatever I may have learned since, my immediate mental picture of the landing is still the Rothermel one.

When the pious and imaginative Mrs. Hemans wrote her Pilgrim poem in 1826 in Rhyllon, Wales, she knew almost

Did the Fathers in 1620 really land on that famous slab of granite? Through the haze of

The PILGRIMS

...with seamanship than with promoting the traditional image of their landing.

verses. Before her poem appeared, the landing of the Pilgrims was scarcely more than a local New England tradition. She expanded it across the English-speaking world, making the landing a national myth.

The subsequent pervasiveness of the myth is the more curious in that from 1620 until 1769 almost no one in Plymouth paid any attention to it. Those obscure dissenters who disembarked from the *Mayflower*—they called themselves "Saints" and did not come to be known as Pilgrims until the nineteenth century—were too preoccupied by the harsh conditions of their arrival to see anything symbolic in their landing. Governor William Bradford in writing his history *Of Plimouth Plantation* ten years afterward never referred to the *Mayflower* by name but merely as "the Ship." Nor does any contemporary account mention a landing on a rock. The first time Plymouth Rock's existence is recorded is in 1715, when it is described in the town boundary records as "a great rock."

Whether or not the Pilgrims actually landed on Plymouth Rock cannot be finally proved one way or the other. It is possible that they did, but much more likely that they did not. Certainly they must have noticed the ten-ton boulder as they approached land. That granite egg laid by the glacier was the most conspicuous object on the flat, curved shore line, a seamark for any helmsman. But even if it lay low enough in the water—and it seems more probable that it then stood above the high-tide mark—it is hard to imagine the helmsman on that bleak, brawling December day taking the risk of battering his craft against it when the wide sheltering inlet of a brook lay only a hundred yards or so beyond. A spot just inside the mouth of the brook—later known as the Town Brook—became the first general landing place, and here a pier was soon built. Plymouth's first street (now Leyden Street) was laid out along the brook's north bank.

That mixed company of forty-one "Saints" and sixty-one "Strangers"* had already spent a month ashore,

nothing about America. The Rhyllon grocer happened to deliver a few purchases to her wrapped in an old newspaper which somehow turned out to have been printed in Boston, Massachusetts. While she was unwrapping her groceries she noticed an account of the 1824 celebration of Forefathers' Day in Plymouth. Until then she had never heard of the forefathers, but, inspired by the crumpled paragraphs, she sat down and composed her

*Saints and Strangers: The leaders of the *Mayflower* group were religious dissenters who called themselves "Saints," and excluded those who did not follow their strict rules of conduct and thought. They caused much trouble at the Plymouth settlement by imposing their views upon the majority, the "Strangers," who sought economic opportunity rather than religious salvation in the New World.

myth that surrounds it, a profound truth may be dimly seen   *By* FRANCIS RUSSELL

and the ROCK

across the bay, before the Plymouth landing. Sixty-five days out of Plymouth, England, the *Mayflower* made her landfall on the outer edge of Cape Cod near the bluffs of Truro, then headed southward, but turned back fearfully at the sinister turbulence of the Chatham shoals. Next morning, Saturday, November 11, 1620,* Captain Christopher Jones rounded the tip of Cape Cod and dropped anchor in what would become known as Provincetown Harbor.

A small advance party of armed men landed to look for supplies of wood and water, marched several uneventful miles and returned with a boatload of juniper branches to fumigate the *Mayflower* from the foulness of the voyage. This was the first landing of the Pilgrims in the New World. Prayers confined the company to the ship on the Sabbath, prayers and the Mayflower Compact—a practical document, whatever its later democratic symbolism, drawn up by the Saints at the time to meet the disgruntled challenge of the Strangers. On Monday morning the women were put ashore under guard to wash great bundles of dirty clothes and bedding. Meanwhile the men set to repairing the longboat, or shallop, which had been stored on the upper deck and was much damaged by the buffetings of the voyage; it would be needed for exploring the coast.

The dune-edged landscape in the fading aftermath of autumn offered "a wether-beaten face, and ye whole countrie full of woods & thickets represented a wild & savage heiw." Yet, Saints and Strangers together knew they must find a place to settle before the winter caught them. When after several days the shallop was still not ready, Captain Myles Standish led a party of twenty, including sixteen volunteers armed with musket and

*The dates given in this article are Old Style, ten days behind the New-Style, Gregorian calendar adopted by Great Britain in 1752.

corselet, down the beach on the first of a series of "Discoveries," as they chose to call their explorations. They had marched about a mile when they saw five or six Indians with a dog in the distance. At sight of the whites the Indians whistled to the dog and darted into the woods. Standish and his men with ignorant valor dashed after them. Fortunately the Indians had not prepared an ambush.

The Englishmen spent a night on the sands shivering with cold and tormented by lack of water. The next morning they lost themselves in a tangle of thickets, but managed to regain the beach; following Indian footprints, they discovered a spring and later came across the heaped mounds of an Indian burial ground. On their way back they found more mounds at the base of a hill, and digging into one newly made, uncovered a large basket filled with some bushels of seed corn plus several dozen red, yellow, and blue ears. The hill they called Corn Hill. The ears they carried back with them, reaching the ship at the end of the third day.

Not for another ten days was the shallop ready, and by that time the first snow had fallen. Twenty-four Pilgrims and nine of the *Mayflower* crew left on the second "Discovery." Heavy seas soon forced the shallop back. Rather than return, however, the Pilgrims waded ashore in the waist-deep water and huddled overnight in driving snow. In the morning they managed to shoot a few geese. On reaching Corn Hill they dug the rest of the corn from the now-frozen ground with their swords and cutlasses and sent it back by the shallop. Wandering as far as Nauset, they came upon conical Indian huts, opened several nearby graves, and removed "sundrie of the prettiest things" that had been buried with the Indian dead. In one they found the body of a yellow-haired man—possibly a Frenchman who had died in captivity. On their

PILGRIM HALL, PLYMOUTH

Half enshrined: *The Rock split when patriots tried to move it in 1774; they put the top piece beside an elm in the town square (left). In 1834 it was taken to Pilgrim Hall, emblazoned with the famous date, and encircled by a protective iron grille (below).*

return the whole company debated about making a settlement at Corn Hill. They decided against it because of the shallow harbor and the lack of water.

The third "Discovery" was to bring the initial landing at Plymouth. Although to the *Mayflower* passengers the land around Massachusetts Bay seemed ominously strange, it was to mariners no *terra incognita*. As early as 1602 Cape Cod had been named by Bartholomew Gosnold, who commanded the first recorded landing of Englishmen in New England. Samuel de Champlain mapped Plymouth Harbor three years later, as did the Dutchman Adrian Block in 1614. Captain John Smith had ranged the New England coast that same year; his map called the harbor Accomack, a name subsequently altered by Charles I to Plymouth. One of the *Mayflower* mates, Robert Coppin, who had been with Smith, persuaded the *Mayflower* company that everything needed for settlement was there—a deep harbor, fresh water, cleared fields, and natural fortifications.

The winter of 1620 was a mild one—the settlers suffered more from damp than cold—but it began with a cruelly frigid spell. When on December 6 the shallop set off across Cape Cod Bay with eighteen men, it was so cold in the open boat that two of them fainted before they reached what is now Wellfleet Harbor. "It frose so hard," Bradford wrote, "ye sprea of ye sea lighting on their coats, they were as if they had been glased." Ten Saints went along, among them William Bradford and Edward Winslow. The others included Captain Jones, first mate John Clarke, Standish, and Coppin as pilot.

They sailed south past Corn Hill and swung around a sandy point into Wellfleet Harbor. Landing, they spent an uneasy night on the beach behind a "barricado" of logs and branches, for Indians had been seen in the distance. Next day they roamed the woods, found another burial ground, and returned to build a second barricado farther up the beach; that night was troubled by one "hideous & great crie."

In the morning while some of the party were eating breakfast around the fire and others had begun to carry their gear to the shallop, a band of thirty to fifty Indians suddenly attacked, lacing the barricado with arrows. Standish was one of the first to fire back at the yelping, painted figures. "Woach! Woach! Ha! Ha! Hach! Woach!" Bradford recorded their war cry. The thundering blunderbusses frightened off the attackers.

There was a sprinkling of sunshine when the shallop pushed off across the bay, but within two hours a snow squall blew up, whipping the glaucous water to foam. Before long, the rudder broke, leaving two men to steer as best they could with oars. The brief afternoon was fading as Coppin made out the encouragingly familiar outline of the thin sandspit that almost surrounded the harbor of Plymouth. The crew pressed on more sail. The mast strained, then finally broke in three pieces. Somehow they managed to cut it away without capsizing, and the wild sea bore them along. The closer the land loomed, the less familiar it looked to Coppin. As they neared the narrow channel at the tip of the spit, he lost his nerve, crying out that his eyes had never seen the place before. The day was saved by a lusty seaman who stuck to his oar and "bade those which rowed, if they were men, about with her, or else they were all cast away."

In the growing darkness they managed to get under the lee of a wooded shore. Remembering the "Woach! Woach!" of the night before, they stuck to the shallop until the cold grew so unbearable that Mate Clarke and several of the boldest finally landed and kindled a fire. The others soon followed. Next morning they found they were on an island—known ever after as Clark's Island—which lay about three miles northeast of Plymouth Rock. The cold spell had broken and the day, a Saturday, was fair. They prepared to keep the Sabbath.

Bradford gives an unembroidered account of the legend-embroidered landing of December 11, supposedly on Plymouth Rock:

On Munday they sounded ye harbor and found it fitt for shipping; and marched into ye land, & found diverse cornfields, & little running brooks, a place (as they supposed) fitt for situation. At least it was ye best they could find, and ye season, & their presente necessitie, made them glad to accepte of it. So they returned to their shippe again with this news to ye rest of their people, which did much comforte their harts.

Nothing about any landing on any rock. On December 15, the *Mayflower* weighed anchor and sailed across the bay. After some difficulties with an adverse wind, she slipped between the sandspits and dropped anchor beyond Clark's Island. On December 18 a landing party under Captain Jones went ashore to explore the country further and to determine on a place of settlement. Where they landed is unknown, but it was probably just within the mouth of the Town Brook.

By Christmas Day (which they did not celebrate, regarding it as a wanton papist holiday), the newcomers were shuttling back and forth between the ship and the shore, and had begun to construct the first mud-and-wattle shelters of what would be the town of Plymouth. The misery of that winter with its alternations of rain and snow left half the company in their graves before the belated New World spring arrived. Years of hunger, frustration, and tragedy were to follow until the survivors could be certain that the Plymouth colony would endure. Such carking years gave the settlers little time or desire to concern themselves with the past when the present still snuffled like a wolf at the door. To have landed and to have endured was enough. Who landed where was of interest to almost no one.

As each early communal settlement gives way to gradations of wealth, the more firmly established inhabitants have the leisure to turn to genealogy and the rediscovery of the past. By the middle of the eighteenth century Plymouth's Old Colony was long since absorbed by Massachusetts, and Plymouth itself had become no more than a quiet county seat. Families like the Winslows and the Bradfords had managed to achieve assured wealth on their outlying estates, but history had moved on to Boston. Not for a century and a half did the descendants of Plymouth's settlers begin to cast a retrospective eye on their ancestors.

Then in 1769 seven young men of Plymouth's first families, disconcerted by "the many disadvantages and inconveniences that arise from intermixing with the company at the taverns in this town," organized the Old Colony Club for genteel association, and voted to commemorate "the landing of our worthy ancestors." They then decided to observe December 22, the New Style anniversary of the original landing, as Forefathers' Day.* The club never consisted of more than thirteen members, and in that time of gathering crisis—the Boston Massacre occurred in March, 1770, only three months after the club's first meeting—the majority were to take the Tory side.

The first Forefathers' Day dinner of the Old Colony Club was held at Loyalist Thomas Southworth Howland's tavern on Cole's Hill and encompassed nine copious courses. The day began with a salvo of cannon in front of the club rooms, followed by the raising of "an elegant silk flag with the inscription 'Old Colony 1620.'" It closed with the singing of John Dickinson's popular ode "In Freedom We're Born" by the boys of the grammar school, an evening of toasts, and a final cannon salvo.

Some time after the Forefathers' Day celebration had become the talk of Plymouth, Deacon Ephraim Spooner, churchman and prosperous hardware merchant, revealed to several members of the Old Colony Club and

*The date was corrected to December 21 in 1849, changed back in 1862, was seesawed back and forth several more times, and is now celebrated on the twenty-first.

to posterity the story of the ancestral landing on Plymouth Rock. Deacon Spooner had heard it in 1741 from the lips of ninety-five-year-old Thomas Faunce, an Elder of the First Church. Faunce in turn had been told about it by his father, John Faunce, who came over in the *Ann* in 1623 and who had presumably heard it first-hand. Although Spooner was only six years old at the time Faunce spoke, he had never forgotten, he said, the words and appearance of the venerable elder.

According to Deacon Spooner, plans had been made in 1741 to build a wharf on the waterfront that would cover a large rock at the base of Cole's Hill. When Elder Faunce heard of this, he had himself carried in a chair three miles to the spot. There, before a large crowd of people, including the six-year-old Ephraim, he pointed out the threatened rock as the very one that his father had assured him had received the footsteps of the forefathers as they landed. The old man "bedewed it with his tears and bid to it an everlasting adieu." Apparently the bedewing had less effect on the builders than it did on Ephraim, for they constructed their wharf as planned, leaving only a small hump of the rock above ground. No one thought more about that encumbering fragment, except for a few cursing carters as they were jolted over it, until the deacon made his revelation a generation later.

As the Revolution loomed up, the members of the Old Colony Club found themselves so divided politically that they disbanded. But the observance of Forefathers' Day continued, and the legend of Plymouth Rock spread. Edward Winslow marked the rock's site on a British survey map of Plymouth made in 1774. Later that year, with the sides now drawn in the coming struggle, the Sons of Liberty—described by the Winslows as the Sons of Licentiousness—were the first to appropriate the rock's burgeoning symbolism. Militia Colonel Theophilus Cotton and a muster of Liberty Boys appeared on the wharf on December 22 with a carriage and thirty yoke of oxen, prepared to take the rock away. They dug down and managed to elevate it from its bed with large screws, but as they attempted to move it onto the carriage it split in two. Some of the more patriotic present saw the split as symbolic of the division between England and the colonies—or so they said afterward. Colonel Cotton and his boys then let the bottom section drop back into its bed, where it remained a few inches above the earth. The top segment, weighing four or five tons, they carted to the Town Square and placed it ceremoniously beside a large elm used to support the newly-erected Liberty Pole which flew their "Liberty or Death" flag.

Forefathers' Day was celebrated each year during the

Half neglected: The stump of the Rock for many years lay imbedded in the surface of a commercial wharf (above left, bottom of picture). Then, in 1859, a monumental canopy was begun (above), to be completed (left) only after the Civil War.

war, but then fell out of use and was not observed again until 1793. John Davis, a Plymouth lawyer, composed an ode for that occasion in which the Rock was for the first time celebrated in verse; the term "Pilgrim" was also used that day in a memorial sermon preached by the Reverend Chandler Robbins. Not for another fifty years would the Forefathers become generally known as Pilgrims, although the term did begin to show up often in the poems and songs written for successive anniversaries.

The name derives from a casual remark of Bradford's in his history. Expressing the regret of the colonists at leaving the city of Leyden in Holland, he wrote: "But they knew they were pilgrimes, & looked not much on those things but lift up their eyes to ye heavens, their dearest cuntrie." Even though Bradford's manuscript was lost in the Revolution (it turned up in 1844 in the library of the Lord Bishop of London and was not returned to Boston until 1897), extracts from it had been copied down, and this unearthed sentence was undoubtedly the impulse that revived the term, just as it later encouraged Victorian illustrators to roll the Pilgrims' eyes heavenward.

Carried along on the new tide of national feeling, the legend of the Rock spread throughout New England. Timothy Dwight, President of Yale, visited Plymouth in 1800, announcing with more emotion than accuracy:

No New Englander who is willing to indulge his native feelings, can stand upon the rock where our ancestors set the first foot after their arrival on the American shore, without experiencing emotions very different from those which are excited by any common object of the same nature.

Two years later the Forefathers' Day address was delivered by no less than John Quincy Adams. But the most imposing celebration came in 1820. For this two-hundredth anniversary, John Watson, one of the few prewar celebrants still living near Plymouth, emerged from his Tory obscurity to organize the Pilgrim Society. A much less exclusive organization than the Old Colony Club, the society opened its membership to everyone with ten dollars "interested in perpetuating the fame of the Forefathers." As an additional honor for the bicentennial Forefathers' Day, a brightly uniformed independent company, the Standish Guards, was organized. Daniel Webster, then at the threshold of his career, appeared resplendently as the principal speaker. Wearing knee breeches, enveloped in a silk gown whose resemblance to a toga was not altogether accidental, and flanked by the Standish Guards, he spoke in front of the rock fragment in the Town Square. For two hours he held forth in ringing Ciceronian periods "full of the farina of thought and feeling," according to a local newspaper, delving rather elaborately into all the sym-

53

bolic meaning of Plymouth Rock. With this celebration the landing of the Pilgrims began to assume a national significance, a significance that Mrs. Hemans would confirm, strengthen, and expand in rhyme six years later.

Unfortunately, as Plymouth Rock increased in fame, it began to decrease in size under the hands of souvenir hunters. Plymouth shops were offering pieces the size of an egg for $1.50, guaranteed to "take a very fine polish." De Tocqueville on his travels noted fragments of the relic in several towns. Finally, on July 4, 1834, what remained of the Rock's upper section was taken from the Town Square and placed in front of the Doric portico of the recently erected Pilgrim Hall. Preceded by schoolchildren and followed by a model of the *Mayflower,* the Rock was carried on a decorated tipcart escorted by the Plymouth Band and the Standish Guards. As the procession was passing the courthouse a linchpin worked out of the cart and the Rock tumbled into the street, breaking into the two pieces so familiar in their cemented state. A year later this portion of the Rock was enclosed by a five-foot-high elliptical fence, the pickets of which were made up alternately of wrought-iron harpoons and boat hooks. The hammered granite base was studded with symbolic scallop shells, and the numerals 1620 were painted on the Rock. Meanwhile the stump on Hedge's Wharf continued to bear the burden of passing wheels. Sometimes, when visitors asked to see it, a clerk would come out of Phineas Wells' adjacent warehouse and brush it off.

In 1859 the Pilgrim Society bought the upper end of the wharf, tore down the warehouse, and laid the cornerstone of a "monumental canopy," designed by Hammatt Billings, over the much-abused base. Its construction was interrupted by the Civil War and finally completed in 1867. Soon after its erection the intrepidity of souvenir hunters forced the addition of iron gates.

For casual visitors to Plymouth it was always a little perplexing to find two Plymouth Rocks, each in a separate enclosure. To end this confusion the Pilgrim Society in 1880 moved the upper section from its metal cage and united it with the stump under the Billings canopy. The Rock, as many noted, was still eight or ten feet above the high-tide mark, but at least it was all in one place. At this time the date, 1620, was carved into the stone to replace the painted numerals.

During the next forty years Plymouth Rock remained secure and unaltered under its baldachin. In 1883 the Pilgrim Society bought the rest of the wharf, leveled the remaining warehouses, and fitted the lower wharf end as a steamboat landing. Then, in 1920, amidst tremendous preparations for the three-hundredth anniversary

of the Landing of the Pilgrims, the wharf was removed, the waterfront re-landscaped, and the canopy torn down.

The Tercentenary Celebration opened on Forefathers' Day, 1920, with an issue of commemorative U.S. stamps. At Plymouth, Governor Calvin Coolidge, the Vice President-elect, made a short address in his appropriately old-fashioned style. Senator Henry Cabot Lodge was the principal speaker. The following week two steam shovels dug around the Rock, which was then wrapped in lengths of chain and hoisted out of its bed. The three sections promptly came apart. They were set aside while the site was excavated down to sea level. A month later the base was replaced, some ten feet lower, and the more familiar upper segment cemented to it. With Plymouth Rock at last located where it could be lapped twice a day by the high tide, a white granite Grecian temple, designed by McKim, Mead and White, was raised over it.

A tercentenary pageant, *The Pilgrim Spirit,* written by Harvard's professor of drama, George Pierce Baker, was performed the next summer. At this climax of the celebration the presidential yacht *Mayflower,* with President Harding aboard, steamed into Plymouth Harbor accompanied by four battleships and six destroyers. On landing Harding spoke as he usually did, with empty resonance. The Grecian temple was finally dedicated the following November on a wild day of rain and wind.

After three centuries the legend of Plymouth Rock has become so fixed in the American consciousness that the Rock itself takes on the magical aura of a Blarney Stone

Reunion: The tercentenary saw commemorative stamps (left), and the reunited fragments of the Rock lowered to water level (above). Right, the Mayflower II *lies at anchor off the Grecian temple now housing the great relic.*

54

or a Stone of Scone. When some prankster in 1937 daubed the Rock with red paint, the news flashed across the country. It seemed a national desecration. At once Harvard University and the Communist Party of Massachusetts publicly disclaimed any connection with such lurid lithography. I remember from my Harvard days a story Professor Howard Mumford Jones told of an old Negro janitor from the University of Texas who made a sightseeing bus tour of the United States. When he reached Plymouth, he sent back a postcard of Plymouth Rock on which he had written: "Here is where our forefathers landed." So we had felt in the Tileston School, even though most of us in that fifth-grade room were—like myself—members of what Boston's Mayor James Michael Curley liked to call the "newer races." I suppose it was the somewhat ponderous piety of the legend, plus childhood recollections of *The Landing of the Pilgrims* framed on a schoolroom wall, that inspired Dorothy Parker's remark in the brittle twenties that it would have been better if, instead of the Pilgrims landing on Plymouth Rock, Plymouth Rock had landed on the Pilgrims.

Yet, if the landing on Plymouth Rock is a myth, it is no more a myth than that the Stone of Scone once served as Jacob's pillow, no more recent a myth than Blarney's gift of eloquence. And behind the myth is a profound truth. In a sense the old Texas janitor was right. Each of us has made his symbolic approach to Plymouth Rock; each is here because someone took a step forward and felt a sustaining firmness underfoot, whether the landing took place from the *Mayflower*, from an Irish "coffin ship," on Ellis Island, or from the last jet at Logan or LaGuardia.

I sense the tenacity of that feeling whenever I visit Plymouth on a bright summer's day. The approaches to the Grecian temple are traffic-blocked. Forty assimilative years have given the white columns a certain minimum of harmony with their nonclassical surroundings. Cars with license plates from every state in the Union are parked for a mile along Water Street. The *Mayflower II,* brave in new paint at her dock, sets off the striated blue of the harbor and the yellow streak of sandspit that almost encompasses it. To the right on the horizon are the bluffs of Manomet, and to the left a single white house breaks the dense greenery of Clark's Island. The crowds are twenty deep around Plymouth Rock. Two college boys in Pilgrim costume alternate in giving talks on the Rock's history, then pass around their wide-brimmed pot hats. Their talks are at least eighty-five per cent accurate. Across the road a goateed photographer, also dressed as a Pilgrim, is waiting to snap the tourists. They in turn may focus their own cameras on him for twenty-five cents a pose. As I wedge my way to the iron guardrail under the pediment and stand looking down at Plymouth Rock in its pit, I feel a homely affection for that familiar, battered granite lump, and I sense a comradeship with those strangers in their summer clothes who have gathered with me to stare at it.

A frequent contributor to American Heritage, *Francis Russell is the author of a recent book on the Sacco-Vanzetti case,* Tragedy in Dedham.

For further reading: Saints and Strangers, *by George F. Willison (Reynal & Hitchcock, 1945)*.

A Sword for George Rogers

In pioneer Kentucky the year 1777 was a desperate time. Across the Ohio, tribal drums were throbbing. From Detroit and from the nearer posts of Kaskaskia and Vincennes the British were arming raiding parties. The paymaster at Detroit was ready to pay for American hair. Just before this "year of the bloody sevens" began, the first scalps were taken at McClelland's Station, a huddle of cabins beside the Royal Spring on Elkhorn Creek. It lay near the Ohio and was most vulnerable. When John McClelland died of a Mingo bullet the settlers crept out of their stockade and hurried through the woods to Harrodstown.

With McClelland's abandoned there were just three stations left—Harrodstown, Boonesborough, and Logan's Station. Harrodstown was the oldest—built in 1775—and it had the largest enclosure and the heaviest log palisade. It was the county seat (Kentucky being a county of Virginia) and the military capital. One of its jutting blockhouses was the frontier Pentagon.

Here George Rogers Clark, aged twenty-four, commanded the defenses. His arsenal was a dozen kegs of powder and some bullet molds. He had a few score woodsmen and hunters, and he had his own boldness.

Clark was a single and a single-minded man. His comrades in Lord Dunmore's War had married, but Clark would never have a wife. He was all for action. He had lived alone in a lean-to on the upper Ohio. He had explored wild land and located future town-sites. Now he was the defender of the western country.

On a spring day in 1777 he called four woodsmen in—Samuel Moore, Ben Linn, Si Harland, and Simon Kenton. Clark wanted information about the British posts at Kaskaskia and Vincennes. It was agreed that two spies would be less suspect than four. They drew lots. That night Linn and Moore slipped out of the fort and headed for enemy country.

Two months later they were back, with a gratifying report: there were no British troops in Kaskaskia; the fort was loosely held; the French inhabitants could be won over easily. That fall Clark traveled to Virginia. In

Far from the war's main currents, a resourceful Virginian set off down the swift Ohio to win its strategic valley for the cause of independence

ILLUSTRATED FOR AMERICAN HERITAGE BY BERNARD KRIGSTEIN

Clark

By WALTER HAVIGHURST

Williamsburg he asked for authority, men, and arms to attack the British posts north of the Ohio. After long debate he was commissioned lieutenant colonel, empowered to recruit 350 men, and allowed $6,000 for ammunition and supplies.

At Redstone on the Monongahela he embarked 150 men in five flatboats, loaded some tons of rotting buffalo meat, and headed west. It was fine weather, mid-May, 1778, with a steady river current. On Corn Island, near the future site of Louisville, he organized his companies and told them of their destination. Some uneasy men deserted, but a file of Kentuckians arrived from Harrodstown. He had about 175 men, but among them were his old comrades Simon Kenton, Joseph Bowman, and Leonard Helm. At daybreak on June 24 they pushed off for Illinois.

The river ran swift and loud below Corn Island. While Clark's four boats were swirling through the "Falls," the day grew dim. Men stared up at a hazy half-disk in the sky. The half-coin shrank to a crescent and a star came out. In a ghostly gloaming the boats swept into deep water. Then the roar of rapids faded and the sun grew bright.

Clark knew enough astronomy to understand that they had witnessed a solar eclipse, but he said nothing to his wondering men. Let it be a solemn moment. They were four small companies invading a vast country. Let them wonder at an omen in the sky.

The site of old Kaskaskia now lies under the wide slow waters of the shifting Mississippi, but in 1778 that French town was the chief settlement in Illinois. French missionaries had established a college there, French traders had built warehouses on the river, French troops had raised stone blockhouses above their timbered fort. Kaskaskia remained French after the British took control in 1765. The *habitants* kept on in the same way, working their ribbon fields, grazing their cattle on the prairie commons, peacefully coexisting with the Indians. The savages went regularly to the mission chapel, crossing themselves at mass, chanting alternately with the villagers at vespers—a couplet of a psalm in Latin followed by the gutteral couplet in Piankeshaw. Periodically they daubed themselves with paint and whooped off for Kentucky.

On that June day in 1778 when the solar eclipse darkened the morning sun, old men in the startled Indian camp thumped ceremonial drums and raised a wailing chant to Mishemenetoc. Then the shadow passed from the prairie, and the sun blazed down. Good Father Pierre Gibault quieted the fears of French and Indians—it was a natural thing and no disaster. A week later, however, as suddenly and silently as the eclipse, the Revolution came to drowsing Kaskaskia.

The British government in that remote place was represented by a Frenchman, Philippe François de Rastel, Sieur de Rocheblave, who had chosen to stay in the West after the French surrender in 1763. He had served in the French Army, helping to defeat Braddock's expedition in Pennsylvania, and had commanded a French post, Fort Massac, on the Ohio. But now he had taken a British command, under appointment of the English king. His small pay was in arrears, and the stingy British government in Canada had disregarded his request for military goods. He had asked to be relieved of his command, but no successor came.

On July 4, 1778, Rocheblave crossed the Mississippi to dine with the Spanish commander at New Madrid. He returned to Kaskaskia that evening, passing through the warm village streets—fiddle music and the sounds of dancing came from an open door—and into his quarters in the riverside stockade. He wrote a letter to Lieutenant Governor Henry Hamilton in Canada before he and Madame de Rocheblave retired.

A few hours later, awakened from sound sleep, he stared at two half-savage figures, a flickering lantern throwing their huge shadows on the wall. George Rogers Clark and Simon Kenton took the commander downstairs in his night dress and informed him that his town was now under the control of Virginia. Outside, one of Clark's captains gave the signal and an uproar began. Through the streets roamed 175 invaders, whooping, roaring, shouting. When lights showed in the windows, Clark's sentries proclaimed the capture of Kaskaskia and warned the citizens to stay within doors until daybreak. Kaskaskia had fallen to the Americans without a gunshot.

For two days, while marching overland from the Ohio River, Clark's men had subsisted on wild berries. That morning, in fear and curiosity, the French housewives provided pork, mush, hominy, beans, potatoes, and the soldiers feasted. Clark then marched his force to the edge of town and posted them there. Back in the village Clark and his captains walked through streets as silent as a ghost town, with the banner of Virginia floating over the fort and the frightened *habitants* peering from their windows. Clark intended no violence to these people, but he was in hostile country and greatly outnumbered. He must keep the villagers frightened and guessing. Evicting a family in the center of town, he made their cottage his headquarters.

57

As the fearful citizens stepped into the streets they saw their settlement encircled by men with long rifles on their shoulders and hunting blades in their belts; Mitchi Malsa —Big Knives—the Indians called them. It was a forbidding name. (With the Indian vocabulary printed in his *Travels*, the eighteenth-century French writer Constantin Volney noted that most words implying beauty and goodness began with *p*, and most *m* words were fearsome.) The Kaskaskians knew that British-armed Indians had harried the Kentucky settlements. Was this a retaliation?

To Father Gibault the villagers looked for guidance. He had told of the uprising of the colonies and their war with the British. Now, leading a committee of six nervous citizens, the priest went to the door of Clark's headquarters. So began Pierre Gibault's familiar role in frontier history.

Inside the room Clark and his captains sat around a bare table. In the warm summer morning they had stripped off their buckskin shirts. Dirty, sweating, scratched by brambles in the river thickets, they looked up at the priest and his delegation. When Father Gibault asked for the commander, a powerful, half-naked man with sandy red hair and a stubble of smoke-stained beard offered a chair. Facing the red-haired colonel, Father Gibault made his request: the citizens of Kaskaskia, British subjects as they were, expected to be separated and carried off as captives, perhaps never to meet again. Might they, before their exile, gather in the church to seek God's blessing?

Clark answered brusquely. They could go to their church if they wanted. He had no objection. But no person was to leave the town. With no other word he dismissed them.

In the chapel the whole village gathered, while certain older citizens recalled how the Acadian French had been driven from their homes in Nova Scotia. The priest tried to quiet these fears; he offered God's blessing, but he could not predict the will of the Big Knives. After an hour they emerged into the silent, sunlit streets. Father Gibault went again to the commander. He found a more civil-looking man; Clark was freshly bathed and in a clean hunting shirt. This time the priest expressed a hope that the French families might not be broken up and that the women and children could be allowed to take with them some clothing and provisions. The citizens, he added, knew little about the American Revolution, and they had never felt like British partisans.

Clark was trying a strategy, and this was the moment he had waited for. After filling the town with fear he could fill it with rejoicing, and so win the gratitude of the French citizens. His manner changed. His mission, he said, was not to cause suffering but to end it. He had come to Illinois not to plunder but to prevent violence. The citizens could remain in their village, in peace and harmony, without fear of danger. Then he added that France had come to the aid of the American colonies; at this moment French ships were bringing men and materials to support the Revolution.

As his words went through the town, joy replaced desolation. Men laughed in the streets, and women carried fresh food to the Virginia troops. When Clark proposed that they take an oath of allegiance, the citizens cheered and sang. In the chapel Father Gibault gave thanks for deliverance and mercy. After less than a day of captivity these British subjects were American citizens. A new future had come to Kaskaskia, which in time would become the capital of the state of Illinois.

That evening Clark sent a troop of men, mounted on French ponies, over the old Fort Chartres Road to Cahokia, sixty miles to the north. Some young citizens of Kaskaskia galloped with them into the sunset. All night they traveled under the summer stars. At dawn the villagers of Cahokia heard a clatter of hooves and looked out at a line of dusty horsemen. The Kaskaskians explained the invasion and urged their neighbors to join the American future. Cahokia, like Kaskaskia, was won without a bullet.

With the American Bottom—the bottom lands at the confluence of the Kaskaskia and the Mississippi—in his control, Clark turned his thoughts across the prairie to Vincennes on the Wabash. From that base the British had armed scores of Indian war parties for raids on the Kentucky settlements. The Illinois country would not be won until he had control of Post Vincennes.

The day after the capture of Kaskaskia Clark sent three scouts, Kenton, Shadrach Bond, and Elisha Batty, to explore the military strength of Vincennes. The three men traveled warily over two hundred miles of prairie. Near Vincennes they hid in a thicket, waiting for darkness. By starlight they crept over the wide grazing common, leaving their rifles and their wide-brimmed Kentucky hats in the rank grass. Wrapped in blankets they strode like Indians through the town. They saw a peaceful place, with no British garrison and no alarm of American invasion north of the Ohio. One visit was probably enough, but spying was an exhilarating mission. The scouts hid outside of town and came back a second night, and a third. Then they turned back to Kaskaskia with their reassuring intelligence.

There, waiting for the spies' report, Clark was employing a strategy based on psychology. He let the citizens know that he was thinking of ordering an army from Kentucky to attack Vincennes. That town was in Father Gibault's parish, and the priest came to Clark with the suggestion that force would not be required. He knew that the British governor was absent, on business in Detroit. He felt that the citizens of Vincennes could be won over to the American side peaceably. He offered to go there to explain the American cause.

The priest set out with a small party of horsemen, including Dr. Jean Laffont, a native of the French West Indies who carried on his medical practice over the huge country of Father Gibault's ministry. Like the priest, the physician had the confidence of the French people. Clark could be assured that it was a persuasive delegation that loped over the prairie.

In two weeks they were back, with good news. The *habitants* of Vincennes were ready to pledge allegiance to America; even the Indian chiefs on the Wabash wanted to smoke the calumet with the Big Knife commander. Clark promptly sent Captain Leonard Helm to treat with the Indians and command the fort at Vincennes. As the summer ended and the prairies withered to autumn, Clark was in control of all the Illinois country.

But the Indians were an uncertain quantity; they feared the advance of the Americans, and they had British encouragement and support. With his single regiment Clark could not fight a dozen tribes, though perhaps he could lure them away from the British. He knew the Indian curiosity and love of council, and he waited for the chiefs to approach him. The overture came at the end of summer; an Indian messenger rode into Kaskaskia telling of a gathering of tribesmen at Cahokia. They wanted to see the chief of the Big Knives and to receive American presents. Clark was ready.

When he reached Cahokia, an impressive sight greeted him. For miles around, the town was encircled by Indian camps. Here were warriors of many nations— Chippewas from the northern forests, blanketed Ottawas from the shores of Lake Huron, Sauk and Foxes from Wisconsin, Miami and Wyandots from beyond the Wabash, and all the prairie tribes of the Illinois people. At night the horizon was ringed with campfires.

Now the young commander drew upon

"Facing the red-haired colonel, Father Gibault made his request..."

all he knew of Indian diplomacy. He listened to the speeches and smoked the feathered pipes. For three days he waited, silent; during that time a party of Puan warriors tried to take his life but were driven off at midnight by Clark's sentries. When their chiefs came to make amends, the Colonel stood at full height outside the doorway of his cottage. "I am a man and a warrior," he said. "I do not care who are my friends or foes." In a later time Clark recalled with wry satisfaction that he "gave Harsh language to supply the want of Men."

The next day he stood above a symbolic fire, holding up two belts of wampum. "I carry in my right hand war"— a blood-red belt—"and peace in my left"—a belt of white. It was for the chiefs to choose. Then, still holding up the belts, he gave a compact history of America, drawing a parallel between the colonists and the native tribes.

They don't know well how to make blankets, powder, and cloth. They live chiefly by making corn, hunting and trade, as you and the French your neighbors do. But the "Big Knives" are daily growing more numerous, like the trees in the woods, so that the land got poor and hunting scarce . . . Then the men learned to make guns and powder so that they did not have to buy so much from the English. They [the English] got mad and put a strong

garrison through all our country (as you see they have done among you, on the lakes, and among the French) and would not let our women spin, nor the men make powder, nor let us trade with anybody else, but said that we should buy all from them—and since we had got saucy, they would make us give them two bucks for a blanket that we used to get for one—and that we should do as they please, and killed some of us to make the rest fear. This is the truth and the cause of the war between us."

Scornfully he told how the English "got weak and hired you red people to fight for them." His eyes moved over the tribesmen. "You can now judge who is in the right. Here is a bloody belt and a white one. Take which one you please."

All night there was dancing round the tribal fires while the chiefs counseled together about the words of the Big Knife. Next day they formed a ring and lighted the fire. A feathered chief advanced, holding the white belt of peace. Another approached with a calumet of white pipestone from the Minnesota quarries. A third brought fire to kindle the pipe. The calumet of peace went to Clark and his captains around the circle of sachems.

That night campfires winked far out on the prairie; the tribes were going home. It was October, Indian summer, and Clark rode back to Kaskaskia through the golden haze of the American Bottom.

Meanwhile word of the capture of the Illinois towns had reached General Hamilton in Detroit. He called warriors from the scattered camps and sent his British captains to dance with them around the war post. On October 7 he embarked a force of 175 British troops and 350 Indians for

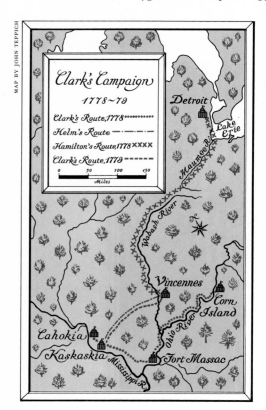

MAP BY JOHN TEPPICH

Clark's Campaign 1778~79
Clark's Route, 1778 ••••••••
Helm's Route —•—•—
Hamilton's Route, 1778 ××××
Clark's Route, 1779 ------
0   50   100   150
Miles

Detroit
Lake Erie
Maumee River
Wabash River
Vincennes
Corn Island
Ohio River
Cahokia
Kaskaskia
Fort Massac
Mississippi R.

Vincennes. They paddled down the Detroit River and crossed the western end of Lake Erie in a curtain of snow. They ascended the Maumee, passed the site of present-day Toledo, and at the end of October, reached the nine-mile portage to the Wabash. With a hundred thousand pounds of stores and ammunition they staggered over the muddy portage. On the way they were joined by two hundred additional warriors. It was a strong frontier army that moved on to Vincennes.

In the Vincennes fort Captain Helm commanded some twenty French militiamen who had come over to the American side. As the British force approached he wheeled cannon into the gate, but there was no alternative to surrender. With Helm as his prisoner, Hamilton took over the fort and quartered his men in the town. As winter came his scouts brought word that Clark had but eighty soldiers in Kaskaskia. It would be easy to crush him, when the weather was right.

Meanwhile Major Bowman, in command at Cahokia, uncovered a British spy whose papers revealed that General Hamilton planned an offensive in Illinois. At this information, Clark stared across the winter prairie. Half his troops had gone back to Kentucky as their terms of enlistment expired. He had no money to pay the men who remained; he could feed them only through the generosity of Kaskaskia merchants who accepted his doubtful Virginia scrip and the faith of Father Gibault, who borrowed from the church tithes to supply the Americans. When Clark thought of Hamilton's army approaching, the American cause seemed as desolate as the winter sky. He could not resist that army, but he did instruct the French-Americans how to act if they were captured. Then he set out for Cahokia, to instruct the citizens there. His party, rocking over a frozen road in two-wheeled carts, stopped for the night at the half-way settlement of Prairie du Rocher. There the hospitable villagers entertained with a ball. Clark could not have felt like dancing, but he talked with French farmers around a smoking punch bowl. Then the door burst open, and a wind-bitten horseman brought a stunning message: General Hamilton was nearing Kaskaskia with eight hundred troops and warriors.

Clark ordered horses with a blanket roll behind each saddle. He might have thought of flight to Spanish ground across the Mississippi, but he was thinking only of Kaskaskia. While the men waited he coached them in a border stratagem; if they found the fort under attack they would blanket themselves like Indians and infiltrate the enemy. At the gate of the fort they would make themselves known to the defenders and join the battle.

While they galloped over the iron road Clark listened for sounds of battle. There was only the clatter of hoofs and the creak of saddle leather. When they reached Kaskaskia the town was sleeping. The timbered gate swung open; the fort was secure. Clark had got there ahead of the enemy.

Before daybreak he set fire to houses adjoining the fort; he would leave no cover for attackers. Aroused citizens roamed the streets while soldiers crouched beside cannon at the portholes. Dawn broke over the silent, snow-patched prairie. Then Clark's spies came in with word that ended the alarm. What had been mistaken for Hamilton's army was merely a scouting force; it had lost its way and was now returning to Vincennes.

Day and night Clark kept sentries patrolling the approaches to Kaskaskia. Late in January they accosted a single horseman who wanted to see the American commander. The visitor was Colonel Francis Vigo, a rich merchant who traded throughout the Illinois country. He had come from Vincennes, and he gave Clark a report of the situation there. General Hamilton was making himself comfortable in the fort with a well-provisioned commissary and a strong garrison. He had sent Indian parties on raids to Kentucky, and some of his regulars had gone back to Detroit. In the spring he would gather his forces and march on Kaskaskia.

In the spring . . . Clark had a bold mind, made restless now by the false alarm of Hamilton's attack. He looked at a map, studying the curve of the Wabash and the lowland approaches to Vincennes. At this moment, he wrote later, he would have bound himself to seven years' imprisonment or slavery to have five hundred troops for a fortnight's service. In fact, even with the Kaskaskia volunteers, he had barely 150 men. Still, he had won the Illinois town not by strength or logic but by audacity. *A desperate situation,* he thought, *needs a desperate resolution. The season being so hostile, no enemy would suppose an attack could come over impassable country. Surprise can outweigh numbers. . . .* That night he called in his captains and told them.

Clark's resolve went through the town like a contagion. New French volunteers joined his depleted regiment. Citizens lugged bundles of food and clothing to the fort. With merchant Vigo's backing, Clark bought a Mississippi flatboat and ordered his men to mount six cannon on its deck. The improvised gunboat, in charge of Captain John Rogers, the commander's cousin, pushed off into the gray current of the Kaskaskia. It would go down the Mississippi, up the Ohio, and up the Wabash to hide in the thickets around Vincennes until the arrival of Clark's regiment. Then it would bombard the fort while the troops attacked. The night before Rogers left, Clark had written

"A chief advanced, holding the white belt of peace. Another approached with a calumet. . . . A third brought fire to kindle the pipe."

a letter to Governor Patrick Henry of Virginia. "—I know that the case is desperate; but, Sir, we must either quit the country or attack. . . . Great things have been effected by a few men well conducted. Perhaps we may be fortunate."

On the next day, February 5, 1779, the regiment drew into formation inside the stockade. When the drums were silent Father Gibault raised his hand in blessing. Clark's men marched out of the gate in a thin, chill rain. The watching townspeople called farewell. In five minutes the little army was on the sodden prairie. It was a smaller force than Clark had counted on—some of his troops had been assigned to the gunboat. There were just 130 men facing an exhausting march and a superior enemy in a timbered fort.

A week out of Kaskaskia they reached the Little Wabash. That minor stream was now a mile-wide flood. Beyond it lay the drowned bottoms of the Embarrass River and then the swollen Wabash itself. They were sixty miles from Vincennes, and over all the desolation a cold rain was falling.

Their march seems incredible now. A third of the men were sick with chills and fever. All were wet, pinched, cold, and wretched. They had no sense of history to nerve them. Not even Clark with his dramatics dreamed that this campaign would be ranked with the great military feats, that his gaunt regiment would be immortal. They were merely miserable men slogging through mud and water, wading waist-deep rivers, building rafts to ferry their sick and their baggage, making cold camps in enemy country.

When they reached the Wabash, nine miles below Vincennes, their rations were exhausted. Here they were to meet the gunboat from Kaskaskia, but the swollen gray river, pitted with rain, was empty.* They made "Camp Hunger," and in the gray daybreak they heard the boom

*Rogers and his men had fallen into an Indian ambush and Rogers himself had been scalped. Clark later found the body.

To the Inhabitants &c of Vincennes, Gen":
Being now within Two Miles of Your Village with my Army, . . . I take this step to Request of such of you as are true citizens and willing to Injoy the Liberty I bring you, to remain Still in your Houses, and those (If any there be) that are friends to the King of England, will Instantly repair to the Fort and Join his Troops and Fight like men. . . . Those that are True friends to Liberty may Expect to be well Treated as such. I once more Request that they shall keep out of the streets, for every person I find in arms on my arrival I shall treat him as an enemy.   G. R. Clark

While the Frenchman returned to town with that

of cannon—the morning gun from Fort Sackville at Vincennes. Chewing the bark of slippery elm to quiet their stomach pangs, the men chopped logs and laced them together with vines. Next day they ferried the Wabash and floundered toward Vincennes. Through mud and misery they struggled on, arms around each other's shoulders. Late in the day the rain ceased, and thin sunlight slanted through bare trees. From a ridge they saw the houses of Vincennes, the timbered church, the heavy-walled fort with five square blockhouses pierced with portholes.

They captured a stray duck-hunter, a Frenchman from the town. Clark opened his baggage, rubbed his stiffened fingers and wrote a letter:

message, Clark had his men chop twenty saplings and raise flags sewed by the women of Kaskaskia. With every seventh man a flagbearer, he started a zig-zag march that gave the appearance of twenty companies. In the winter dusk they entered the town. At the log church they broke lines and crept under the bastion towers of the fort; the British cannon swiveled but could not tilt. When Clark gave the order his men fired through gaping palisades.

All night the fighting flowed and ebbed and flowed again. Clark's strategy was to spread confusion and bewilderment; he kept his men moving, firing from various quarters, whooping like savages. The French citizens came out with bread, meat, and cheese. With food in their stomachs Clark's men yelled like demons. But coolly they continued pouring their rifle fire through the gun ports. One by one the British cannon were silenced.

Firing slackened at dawn, and Clark sent a message under a white flag to the bastion gate. It was addressed to General Hamilton.

Sir:

In order to save yourself from the Impending Storm that now Threatens you, I order you to Immediately surrender yourself, with all your Garrison, Stores, etc., etc., for if I am obliged to storm, you may depend upon such Treatment as is justly due to a

noon, and a British messenger came out. A curt exchange led to a meeting in the log church: General Hamilton agreed to surrender at ten o'clock the next morning.

That day, February 25, was clear. At mid-morning a company of Clark's mud-stained men drew up at the timbered gate. The British ranks marched out, and Clark's gaunt regiment moved in. They fired the cannon thirteen times, for the thirteen colonies that had become the American nation which now was master of the entire Ohio Valley.

Colonel George Rogers Clark, twenty-five years old, was at the peak of his career.

"...miserable men slogging through mud and water, wading waist-deep rivers, building rafts for their sick"

Murderer beware of destroying Stores of any kind, or any papers or letters ... in your possession, or hurting one house in the Town, for by heavens if you do there shall be no Mercy shewn you.

G. R. Clark

When the messenger brought an answer Clark read it with narrowed eyes.

Gov.r Hamilton begs leave to acquaint Col. Clark that he and his Garrison are not disposed to be awed into any action unworthy of British subjects.

H. Hamilton

Clark gave the word, and firing was resumed. Crouching in ditches and under makeshift barricades, the men fired through gaping timbers. The sun broke through at

Three years after the capture of Vincennes the West was quiet, and the Revolution was over. When Clark returned to Kentucky from a campaign against the Ohio tribes, peace talks had begun in Paris. To Kentucky came an official commission, sent from Richmond to settle Clark's accounts. Clark had received no pay for five years; neither had the men in his command. The commissioners had a bewildering task, checking piecemeal ledgers and sorting chits and promises signed by one officer or another. They worked through this maze of papers and made their report. But nothing was paid: Virginia passed the debt to the federal government, where it rested. In the end Clark got a grant of land, which was promptly claimed by his creditors—holders of vouchers he had signed for military stores. The claimants held Clark responsible, and the law sustained them. There went his land.

The commission had officially approved Clark's own claim for five years' pay and for reimbursement of funds advanced to buy flour for his troops—a total claim of about $15,000. But the state of Virginia declined to make payment without the required vouchers. Clark had delivered his papers to the commission, which sent them on to Richmond. There they were lost.*

For thirty years Clark had no home of his own, though he conquered territory that gave homes to multitudes. At last, in the autumn of his life, he built a log house on the north side of the Falls of the Ohio. So he became a citizen of the Northwest Territory which he had won for his country.

The house stood on a hill looking down at Corn Island,

*They stayed lost for 130 years. In 1913 a pile of documents was found in an attic of the Virginia statehouse. They were the Clark papers—thousands of them. Some were official sheets and ledgers; more were jottings on scraps of paper, even on sandpaper and old playing cards. The past smoulders like an old campfire in those makeshift records: "for four pair handcuffs... for a colt lost when his mare was in public service... ½ gal. rum for a fatigue party landing boats... 6 days board for an Indian interpreter . . . for rum at a treaty . . . for shirts and shoes for Indians . . . 2 lbs. of nails . . . tallow for candles . . . flags for Indians . . . for subsistence for wounded soldiers." Now they are historic treasures, protected from dust, damp, and daylight in the Virginia State Library.

where the commander had drilled his little army for the great campaign. In his first season there a white pirogue steered in to Clark's landing, and two young men climbed the hill. They were William Clark, his youngest brother, and Meriwether Lewis, on their way to St. Louis to recruit men for an exploration to the Pacific. Three years and one month later, in November, 1806, they climbed the hill again, browned and hardened, back from their discovery. They talked of the great plains and the shining mountains, while Clark stared into the fire. He had crossed one wilderness; his tall young brother had completed the journey that led from Virginia to Oregon.

On a winter day six years later a messenger from Virginia brought word of an annual pension of $400 in appreciation of Clark's services. Then across the arms of Clark's roll chair he laid a sword of honor. Its blade was engraved: "Presented by the State of Virginia to her beloved son, General George Rogers Clark, who by the conquest of Illinois and St. Vincennes extended her empire and aided in the defense of her liberties." This was in 1812, and Clark was half paralyzed. His sword hand was dead.

He died in 1818, the year Illinois became a state, still paralyzed and sunk in poverty. But one of his land claims remained—a large tract at the junction of the Tennessee and Ohio rivers; it still belonged to the Indians and could not be seized by Clark's creditors. When the westernmost part of Kentucky came into U.S. possession, the Clark claim proved valid. The old commander was dead, but on that land William Clark founded the town of Paducah.

From this hill above the river George Rogers Clark had watched the great migration. He saw the future taking possession of the valley. But he could not have pictured a construction of the 1950's. On a vanished canebrake in his Paducah land rose a plant more massive than a fortress and more intricate than a battleship. Today its gaseous diffusion process, monitored by thousands of instruments, produces enriched uranium for the U.S. Atomic Energy Commission.

"A sword of honor . . . 'presented by the State of Virginia to her beloved son. . .'"

Walter Havighurst, research professor of English at Miami University in Ohio, has written a number of books dealing with the region between the Ohio River and the Great Lakes, most recently The Heartland: Ohio, Indiana, Illinois, *published by Harper and Row in their Regions of America series.*

For further reading: Background to Glory: The Life of George Rogers Clark, *by John Bakeless (Lippincott, 1957);* The Life of George Rogers Clark, *by James Alton James (University of Chicago Press, 1928).*

READING, WRITING, AND HISTORY

By BRUCE CATTON

A Haunted Half-World . . .

The border line between the known and the unknown is very hazy. History is in one compartment, legend and myth are in another, and between the two there is an undiscovered world whose margin, as Tennyson remarked, fades forever and forever as we move. We know a little of our past, and much less of our future; somewhere between what we know and what men who lived before us have dreamed, there is a haunted half-world out of which we can never quite make sense but which we can never possibly ignore. We are bounded in myth and legend, and it is never really possible for us to determine just what we know and what we wish that we knew.

Who knew about America, for instance, before anyone had given the place a name or really seen it? Why is that word magical? Just where, before history had its dawn, did someone know about it, touch its shores,

---
Land to the West: St. Brendan's Voyage to America, by Geoffrey Ashe. Viking Press. 352 pp. $6.75.
---

and make out of it something that stirred the pulse and quickened the imagination? Was all of this just a figment of the imagination, or did someone—centuries before Columbus—know something that got lost in the mist of prehistory?

Probably we will never know; yet the business is unsettling, arousing the imaginative faculty, stirring queer racial memories that touch our vision of the future rather than of the past. We look ahead when we look backward. What we really know may matter less

than the haunting things that make us wish we knew, the stray hints that cannot quite be brushed aside: the racial evidences that people went farther and found out more than they were ever able to admit.

Thus: did the Irish get to America before Columbus, before the Vikings, before any solid historical record? Maybe not, and it does not make much difference if they did; yet more than a thousand years ago someone knew something about what lay beyond the Atlantic mists, and if what they knew got buried in myth and legend, the important fact now is that they did know *something*. That simple fact makes us restless. How did they find out about it?

Hunting for the answers to such questions is like exploring the matter of just what songs the Sirens sang, to which there is no positive answer. But the quest is worth-while, and Mr. Geoffrey Ashe, an inquiring Englishman who has the happy faculty of doubting that anything is really impossible, looks into it in a completely fascinating little book, *Land to the West*, which is a modest inquiry into the question of whether the Irish had seen and known America half a millennium or more before Columbus sailed.

Mr. Ashe begins by examining the legend of Saint Brendan, who is said to have gone a-voyaging in early medieval times and to have found a strange continent beyond the western ocean before the Vikings even got to Greenland. Did Saint Brendan get there or did he not? What is the evidence?

Ireland had seagoing monks and anchorites, as Mr. Ashe remarks, as early as 600 A.D. They went island-hopping, impelled partly by missionary zeal and partly by a yearning for solitude—the same sort of impulse that drove the Egyptian hermits into the emptiness of the deserts of North Africa. They were, at that time, the best scholars in western Europe, they had a solid knowledge of geography, and they wanted to know what lay beyond the sunset. Did they just dream, or did they know something?

The evidence is mixed and contradictory. Early in the Christian era, Irish monks clearly prowled through the outlying islands in their flimsy coracles, going from landfall to landfall and embellishing their accounts with the richness of imagination that goes with Celtic storytelling. But sometime before the Vikings had got to Greenland, a body of lore about Saint Brendan had developed. Instead of a coracle he had an ocean-going ship made of wood, and the stories tell how he went forth, a month or more from land to land, going down the sunset path, and finding a strange earthly paradise far to the west.

As Mr. Ashe emphasizes, this legend probably does not tell about a real voyage; yet it seems to be based on genuine knowledge of such voyages. It is not like the earlier legends, where men hourly discovered new islands; it is full of details about distances, directions, landfalls, and times: somewhere back of it there does seem to be the discovery of a continent. It is a fantastic of the map of the Atlantic, and no one needs to believe the fantasy—and yet the map, somehow, is a good one. Whoever put these legends into writing knew something about the western ocean, about its currents and perils and distances. Brendan may not have been a pioneer, but he was (as Mr. Ashe says) a good listener; and he had been listening to someone who knew something.

"To take the legend seriously," says Mr. Ashe, "is not to make Brendan the discoverer of America, but to remove the discovery back beyond him." It seems to Mr. Ashe that when this story is followed down far enough, one is almost obliged to embrace the theory that someone actually crossed the Atlantic before the tenth century.

On a quest of this kind one never encounters certainty. On the other hand, one never quite encounters absolute disbelief either. The reality behind myth and legend is notoriously insecure—and yet, in the last analysis, myths and legends do not always come out of a complete vacuum. In his search for a proper background, Mr. Ashe goes far afield—even to the legends of the Lost Atlantis, to the odd tales which hang about the sea-wanderings of the early Phoenicians, to the mid-American tales of Quetzalcoatl and his emergence from (and final departure into) the eastern sea, to the queer legends in meso-America of bearded white men who came, stayed, and then vanished, and, first and last, into the deep body of Irish legend which says

that people went west, saw something, and sent back stories about it.

Nothing at all can be proved. There is no certainty anywhere. And yet—as Mr. Ashe says, "there is something there." The infinite mystery beyond the horizon of the western ocean had been touched, just a little, had been explored by men who—heaven only knows why, or how—went on a voyage fully as perilous and hair-raising as the ventures of our present-day astronauts, and came back to tell, as best they could, what they had seen.

We live in a good time for this sort of discussion. We too are poised on the edge of a stupendous jump-off. Our own horizons are being expanded, and the final effect upon us will be just as epoch-making as was the final effect, on men six hundred years ago, of the discovery that off beyond the gulf there is a land that ought to be explored and known. Just at the moment when we have felt ready to give way to despair, an outer door is swinging open. We face what Columbus himself faced: not so much the task to see what lies beyond the outer limits of human thought as to see just what it is, to bring back evidences of it, and to enable mankind to take one more long leap into the perilous, dismaying, and infinitely rewarding unknown.

. . . and the Fight to Own It

It is true, of course, that once the leap is made the things that may immediately come of it are expensive, disillusioning, and (for the time being, at least) very costly. Irishmen, Vikings, and Heaven knows who else had a look at America. What they had seen, other men set out to exploit, and their exploitation turned out to be somewhat bloody. The number of men who died trying to find America is much less than the number who died trying to determine who was going to own America once it had been found, and the moment of vision was followed by a long period in which it became painfully evident that the way of the explorer is much less costly than the way of the exploiter.

As a sample, there is *The French and Indian Wars*, by Edward P. Hamilton, which tells of the desperate struggle for North America waged by the French and English people who came over to have a good go at the marvelous land which the explorers had opened.

Mr. Hamilton retells the story of the way the French and English fought to determine final ownership of the land which is now the United States. It is not really a very pretty story, and Mr. Hamilton does not try to dress it up very much. The Indians themselves, the aboriginal inhabitants who, whatever happened, were going to be dispossessed, do not show up in his pages as the Noble Red Men of tradition. They were stone-age men obsessed with the desire to inflict pain, given to cannibalism, valiant only when the odds were on their side, given to hanging back to see how a battle would go before they came frolicking in with knives and tomahawks to scalp, maim, and sometimes actually to boil and eat the luckless ones who were defeated.

Nor do the contending whites come off a great deal better. The stupidity of the British, who finally won, seems to Mr. Hamilton to be only slightly less than the stupidity of the French, who were at last beaten. The French had the game in their hands and finally gave it away simply because what happened in North America was no more than an echo of the power game that was going on in Europe.

Yet there is a little more to it than that. This continent, this immense expanse which finally would become Pittsburgh and Ohio and Detroit and the bewildering busy industrial nexus which we know today, was then emptiness: virgin land, waiting to be entered, a country of strange beauty and quietness and infinite space, grown noisy and crowded now, empty then, lying at the feet of the men who crossed the ocean to use it.

The men who came over here fought, for more than a century, fought without conscience and without pity, to see who would finally have title to this land. They knew no more what they were fighting for than the early explorers knew what they were discovering. They knew only that this immense vacuum pulled them, a country to be taken, possessed, and—as well as might

---

The French and Indian Wars, by Edward P. Hamilton. Doubleday & Company. 318 pp. $5.95.

---

be—developed, while the new tribe of Americans moved on their way to the future.

We are the heirs of all of this now, and to look back is to see ourselves in the process of taking shape. The fury, the cruelty, the sharp acquisitiveness, that actuated the men who fought their way through the French and Indians Wars are part of us today; so, for a saving grace, is the noble vision that had power over them, the vision of what might some day be done with the infinite land they were fighting for. These qualities are still with us. The end of the story is something we ourselves will tell.

The Courtship of Woodrow Wilson CONTINUED FROM PAGE 31

me unspeakably grateful to know that I have won your *first* love and won it so completely, by I know not what attractions. I am really, then, the only man you ever met that you thought you *could* love? . . .

Are you thinking, my love, as you read this, that you were *not* the first to win *my* love? And did I guess right when I guessed that what you were hesitating to ask was about a certain un-named lady of whom I told you once as we walked by the railroad? Well . . . to make the asking easy (if you want to ask) I'll volunteer one piece of information, which is that I never knew what love was until I knew you, and that, if it was love that I felt for the character which I supposed that lady to possess, it was a very contemptible dwarf beside the strong passion that is now at large in my heart and which leaps with such tremendous throbs of joy at the thought of your love. You need not shrink from hearing me speak of what I have hitherto taken for love: for no woman, my darling, ever had more entire love given her than I have given you . . .

Slowly, and with frequent relapses, Ellen's courage grew. She never again called Woodrow her "Dear Friend." And, when her own words embarrassed her, she let the great poets she knew so well speak for her.

East Rome, Oct. 2, 1883

This morning brought me at once your two letters—of the 27th and 29th—and therefore this day has been like the day on which I last wrote, "high holiday." "All its moments lightly shaken sow themselves on golden sands."

I wonder if you would laugh, or what you would say, if you knew how perfectly daft your letters make me! But no-one could be expected to receive such letters and keep very cool . . .

The ring also came this afternoon. It is a *perfect beauty* in every respect. . . . I can't tell you, my darling, how much I prize it. You are very, very, good—but are you not also very extravagant? Please excuse my impertinence, but really I was startled and amazed at the unexpected apparition of a *diamond.* You know it is not absolutely necessary to wear that particular sort of ring in order to "feel engaged."

. . . I was writing to Beth [a school friend] the other night—about *you* . . . I could honestly say that I had found my—yes, I must say it—my "ideal," though I am a little out of humour with that much abused word. Now I know you will laugh at me, but it is so! Why even those lines which Beth and I selected together, years ago, as best expressing our ideal were written for you! I never saw so perfect a description of anyone. A "jersey" jacket couldn't fit more closely! You may remember the words, for with calm audacity I once quoted them to you myself, knowing that you could not read my thoughts as I did so.

"A mouth for mastery and manful work
A certain brooding sweetness in the eyes,
A brow the harbour of grave thought."

She wore the ring on her right hand because they agreed to keep their engagement a secret from everyone except their families and intimate friends.

Woodrow had never been able to talk to anyone about himself, but now, because he was afraid that Ellen would be disappointed if she did not know in advance exactly what sort of man he was, he wrote the first of many letters of self-revelation.

> Baltimore, Oct. 2nd, 1883
>
> . . . I dreamed about you all last night, my darling. . . . That was a joyous dream . . . I woke up laughing. I had been doing in the dream what I have never done in reality; had been showing you a side of my disposition that you have never seen. I dreamt of the jolliest frolic that we had together . . . and so it was that I awoke in glee. You don't know what a goose I can make of myself upon occasion, when I am with people of whose esteem I am sure and who will think no less of me for my nonsense. Can you love me in my every humour? or would you prefer to think of me as always dignified? I am afraid it would kill me to be always thoughtful and sensible, dignified and decorous.

Ellen's letter of October 2 did not, for some reason, arrive for a week. Then he wrote,

> Baltimore, Oct. 9, 1883
>
> My own darling,
>
> I did laugh at the idea of being your "ideal" (because I am such very gross stuff out of which to construct an ideal!) but my amusement was mixed with another feeling which was the predominant one—with keen delight at the assurance that your love for me is great enough to overlook my faults and weaknesses and enthrone me in your gentle heart . . .
>
> Do you know, dearest, that I am sometimes very much embarrassed when writing to you? I don't mean that I am ever embarrassed in the ordinary sense, but that I am at a loss to know how to express myself. Here's the difficulty: my inclination is to be "making love" in every sentence . . . No term of endearment could run beyond the reality of my feelings: *but one can't convey vocal tones to the written sheet,* and I have as great an aversion from "sweet talk" as from set and formal expressions of affection. . . . There are no words which can express the sentiment of a kiss. A kiss is one of the gestures of that unspoken language which is often so much more eloquent of the deeper and subtler feelings than are any spoken words. . . .

Ellen's next letter contained some playful but searching questions about the "unnamed lady" Wilson had mentioned.

> East Rome, Oct. 6, 1883
>
> . . . Your charming letter of the second full of dreams and other good omens was received yesterday. You dear, delightful boy! I don't think I am dreadfully shocked at any of the

Can you love me in my every humour? or would you prefer to think of me as always dignified?

revelations it contains and I faithfully promise to love you in your every humour. . . .

> Now, . . . I will play jealous and ply you with questions. So you will inform me, Sir, if you please, who the girl was and when and where and how and why and wherefore—the beginning and the end! Was the wound entirely healed before last summer and did it leave a very deep scar? Are you sure there isn't the *least* little rankling pain remaining? . . .

A full account of Woodrow's first love reached her promptly.

> Baltimore, Md., Oct. 11th/83
>
> . . . No young man lives a complete life who is not lifted out of himself by love for some woman who stands to him for a type of what is pure and lovely. . . . it was with that feeling that I met, at Auntie's house, the girl [a first cousin] I came to think entitled to that store of affection. . . . I had about made up my mind beforehand to fall in love with her, and afterwards it seemed an easy enough thing to do. During the next winter (for she was then at home in Ohio) we corresponded regularly and quite voluminously, and, in the summer of 1881 . . . I went out to Ohio to make her a visit; and it was during that visit that I completed the little drama by proposing to her and being refused. . . .
>
> Before last summer came all traces of the wound she had given me were gone. No scar remained anywhere but on my *pride,* which winced a little at the memory of the huge mistake I had made with such wilful blindness. . . .

But Ellen was hurt by Woodrow's story of his first love. She had not known that he had asked the girl to marry him, and she thought that he must have been blindly in love to propose to a first cousin. She wrote what must have been a rather stern letter, because, judging by his reply, it frightened Woodrow.

> Baltimore, Oct. 18th, 1883
>
> . . . My dear sensitive girl seems to have been a good deal shocked by some of the revelations drawn out by her questions. . . . Was it because she was not prepared to receive conclusive evidence that her "ideal" was, after all, a very weak, foolish fellow?
>
> Did you think that I had invited your questions as I did because it would be pleasant to answer them? Very far from it. I invited them because I wanted to have no secrets to keep from you. It would break my heart, my precious Ellie, to lose your love—I could not now live without it—but it would break it quite as surely to have you imagine me wiser

and better than I am and afterwards discover that you had been mistaken. . . . It *was* weak and silly in me to do so "unfortunate" a thing. . . . But, happily, all that is now passed by, and as if it had never happened. I am not a boy any longer. It was left for you to teach me the vast, the immeasurable difference between a youth's fancy and a man's overmastering love. Why, my darling, I am sometimes absolutely frightened at the intensity of my love for you.

And so the difficulty was cleared up. Woodrow plunged harder into his work, although, as he told Ellen, he found it very distracting to be so much in love: "How can a fellow in Baltimore write a lecture on Adam Smith when he's forever thinking of a girl in Georgia?"

Occasionally there were pleasanter alternatives than Adam Smith:

> Balto., Md., Nov. 13th, 1883
>
> . . . We had a very jolly time, and I am afraid that I was not as dignified as I might have been. The company consisted of the young lady aforesaid, her two sisters, a young damsel from Philadelphia, Miss Woods and two of her brothers, and one or two other men besides myself. We compounded the caramels in the dining-room, boiled them in the kitchen, and ate them in the parlour; but before these numerous stages had passed I had had numerous frolics with the young lady aforesaid and had been three times locked up in the pantry, each time gaining my freedom by making demonstrations toward demolishing the larder, and once having one of the young ladies as a fellow-prisoner. I don't always misbehave so when I go out in company; but candy making is scarcely an occupation requiring much dignity. . . .

Christmas of 1883 found the lovers still separated. Woodrow had to stay in Baltimore to study for examinations, while Ellen was now living in Savannah with her grandparents. The only indulgence Woodrow allowed himself during the holidays was to write to her every day instead of every other day. He wore himself out with overstudy:

> Balto., Jan'y 4, 1884
>
> . . . I was both exhausted and intensely nervous and I am just now beginning to feel like my old self again. The last day or two I have been restlessly wandering about trying to bridge over a sort of enforced idleness, the most interesting results of my half-crazy condition having been three successive all-night dreams of you. The first visions were delightful, but in the last from which I awoke only a few hours ago and which still haunts me, *I dreamt that you were dead—* you, without whom I would not care to live, nay, whose loss would make me wish to die. . . .
>
> Interpreted by the accepted canons of superstition, even that terrible dream of last night brings a delightful prophecy

of marriage, which ought to remove one of my chief causes of anxiety . . . namely, the uncertainty of my prospects. . . . I always felt a sort of calm, uncalculating assurance of my ability to make successful shift to support myself; but now that the time for the realization of my sweetest hopes depends upon my securing a good position, I begin to feel very keenly the uncertainty of the prospect. I know what you would say, my darling; I have a perfect assurance of your love and of your willingness to abide the chances of my fortune; but I am none the less eager to make our engagement as short as possible. . . .

Woodrow was in great demand as a speaker, and sometimes indulged in mild boasting about his successes in his letters to Ellen. She wrote:

> Savannah, Georgia
> Mar. 13, 1884
>
> . . . I am very glad that Mr. Wilson, the critic, was so enthusiastically received. I envy the Hopkins Debating Club —lucky fellows that they are! I am wild to hear you speak, perfectly frantic! You wouldn't treat me as Mac does Rose, would you? She has never heard him preach, though everyone else in Sewanee has. He won't let her. . . .

Woodrow replied:

> Balto., Md., March 18, 1884
>
> . . . So you envy the Hopkins Debating Club and are "wild" to hear me speak? . . . I must disappoint you by telling you that I entirely sympathise with "Mac" in being violently opposed to having my sweetheart hear me speak in public. . . .
>
> Of course I don't mean that I intend always to avoid letting you hear me. I mean that I will do nothing to make an occasion for you. . . . There is, on such occasions a terrible wear and tear on the speaker which I attribute to the fact that he has someone besides himself to carry through the race: that there is a heart beating as intensely as his own for his success.

It was the fashion in those days for lovers to exchange locks of hair. The girls wore them in lockets; the men carried them in their wallets. Ellen and Woodrow did not scorn such sentimentality, although they did smile at it. Woodrow wrote:

> Balto., Md., April 1st, 1884
>
> . . . About the dark integument enclosed I have several remarks to make. It is not long enough to hang oneself with, but it is quite visible enough to serve as a fair specimen of the head from which it came. Again, on the one hand, it is an astonishingly small product of two months' persistent culture, though it represents locks long enough to get into their unhappy owner's ears and abundant enough to give him a desperately poetical aspect. . . . But, fortunately the value of this gift depends not on its size, nor upon the

mechanical skill with which it was prepared. It has no intrinsic beauty or worth as have the beautiful silken strands you gave me. . . .

Ellen Axson's father died on May 29, 1884. The sad occasion of the funeral brought Woodrow to Georgia for a two-week visit. After his return to his parents' home in Wilmington, North Carolina, Ellen was busy packing her father's belongings for removal from the parsonage at Rome. Trying hard to be cheerful, she wrote:

> Rome, Georgia, June 28th, 1884
> . . . I have had such a week of it that writing to you seemed, like all the other pleasures of life, "a thing to dream of, not to do;—something forever out of reach" . . . Such a task as it is! And the books are the worst of all. I didn't suppose that anything could make the sight of books so hateful to me. I feel rather spiteful in thinking of the authors! They might have been better employed. I am even inclined to think that—say—three volumes would contain all that was worth saying in the whole lot. . . .
>
> I was very glad to know that you had a pleasant journey and that you hadn't "the blues." That's right, and I shall try to follow your good example. Indeed, I don't think that any thought of *you*—even the thought that you are not here—has power to give me the blues. I am too glad that you are *somewhere!*

Woodrow had asked Ellen to visit him at Wilmington, but her old-fashioned grandmother had refused permission: it would not, she thought, be proper. Obedient Ellen therefore declined the invitation, much to Woodrow's distress:

> Wilmington, June 29th, 1884
> My own darling,
> . . . I could not beg even a friend with such persistent reiteration, but I can beg you . . . to reconsider your refusal to visit Wilmington. . . . There is nothing here, dearest, from which your bashfulness need shrink; nothing but love and love's consideration: and I think that you would face a great deal more than a transient embarrassment for my sake. . . . We have set our hearts on having you come to us. Can you refuse? . . .

The matter was happily settled when Mrs. Wilson wrote to Mrs. Axson, and the old lady relented. The wife of a minister knew, apparently, just what to say to a minister's wife.

> Wilmington, July 13th, 1884
> My sweet Eileen [this was Woodrow's private name for Ellen],
> Hurrah! I knew Mrs. Axson, after all, better than you did, my darling. You may imagine the delight with which I heard dear mother read the enclosed! I went down to the P.O. to mail the letter to my sweetheart which I finished about half an hour ago, and brought from the office this delightful note from Mrs. Axson, in which the dear lady actually expresses the wish that you should visit us! My darling, I can't tell you how happy this has made me because . . . it assures us of having you with us during propitious September. What strides I can take tomorrow in essay "No. 4!" How impossible it will be for headaches to come or for appetite to go: For Sept. is coming!

Meanwhile, Woodrow was hard at work; but he found it difficult to concentrate because Ellen did not write as often as he did.

> Wilmington, July 13th, 1884
> . . . So you "can't take it in" that *your* letters *could* "make such a difference to anyone," can't realize that anybody's life stops for want of a letter from you and want to know if you're "*really* to believe" that my not hearing has such an effect upon my spirits? Well you *are* a little goose, a very desirable and surpassingly lovable little goose, with whom one would wish to live all his life, but a goose for all that, about some things. . . . The simple truth, Miss, in my case, is that if the intervals between your letters be long—and how long a few days seem now!—or if a letter confidently expected at a particular time is in the least bit delayed, everything in my arrangements gets off its hinges: I can't write a single sentence about the Senate, can't be decently sure of an appetite—am a nuisance to myself, and doubtless to everybody about me. . . .

Sometimes Woodrow expatiated on his favorite topics in his letters to Ellen. One of them was oratory:

> Wilmington, Aug. 7th, 1884
> . . . Those people who talk about the press having superseded oratory simply shut their eyes to the plain evidences to the contrary exhibited in all parts of the world. . . . I never yet read a great speech without regretting that I had not heard it. . . . I have read nearly all the published speeches of John Bright . . . but does that compensate me for never having been within sound of the voice of the greatest of living English orators? But hold on, my dear Woodrow! All this argument you are rushing into may be very good, but it is altogether gratuitous. There's nobody on the other side. . . . Let's have a little peace and quiet in a letter! . . .

More typically, he wrote page after page telling Ellen how much he loved her. At the end of a long letter devoted entirely to this subject, he added:

> Wilmington, Aug. 26, 1884
> . . . In looking over this letter, I am constrained to recognize the fact that it is really scandalous. You have enough love talked to you to spoil all the least spoilable girls in a kingdom! My next letter shall be all about the stupidest

news of the town, about parties and fires, political meetings and baseball games, market prices and novelties in ship-rigging. Or else it shall be redolent with all the most pungent thoughts of certain (would be) famous essays now in progress. Look for it with fear and trembling! . . .

Ellen made a great hit with the Wilson family when, in September, she came to Wilmington. At the end of that month she went to New York to study art, and found, after days of searching, a room in a boarding-house on West Eleventh Street which suited her. The rent was low, the landlady a southerner, and the other boarders eminently respectable. She went happily to work at the Art Students' League, and began to enjoy some of the cultural diversions of the metropolis. Woodrow was back at Johns Hopkins, and they were now able to spend weekends together from time to time.

It can-not be chance that brought us together. Sure-ly a man and woman who can love each other as we love must have been born, for each other.

Balto., Oct. 22nd, 1884

My own darling,

It was *terrible* to have to come away! I didn't know *how* terrible it was until the parting was over. I won't say that the pain of separation was greater than the joy of being to-gether—because it wasn't. That joy is beyond all measure, is worth all that can be paid for it. But the leave-taking *is a big price.* . . . And I was brought away with such unrelent-ing vigor that one might have imagined that the railroad authorities knew the temptation I was under to turn back and were determined to give me no chance to do so. We made never a stop between Jersey City and Philadelphia, making those hundred miles in two hours!

Again and again in the fall of 1884, Woodrow comes back to the question of his career and his ambition to be more than a cloistered scholar:

Balto., Md., Nov. 8th, 1884

. . . You'll never find in a *cloister* a fulcrum for any lever which can budge the world!

Here's the problem, then: How get fresh air in this world of book-research? How learn to ride a live horse on a hobby-horse? How discover by reading heavy books the quick, di-rect, certain way to inform and influence men who read only entertaining books—books which touch with a prac-ticed hand their own ordinary lives—books which can be understood without conscious effort? I want to write books which will be read by the great host who don't wear spec-tacles—whose eyes are young and unlearned! I don't care how much contempt may look upon my pages through pro-fessors' glasses! . . .

Ellen was much pleased with her life in New York and the character of her fellow boarders, who had formed a reading group.

New York, Nov. 11, 1884

. . . Mr. Goodrich read from Bret Harte's stories, while Miss M. and I sketched her cousin and Mrs. Jenkins. Mrs. J. is perfectly lovely! and so is Mrs. Weiler! ! and so is Mr. Goodrich! ! ! his loveliness consisting in the fact that he is going to take me to see Irving and Ellen Terry. To go out with a boarding-house acquaintance isn't exactly what I should have anticipated doing; but it hasn't taken a whole month, by any means, to obtain satisfactory evidences as to Mr. Goodrich's character and antecedents. He is a thor-ough gentleman, born and bred—of good old Mass. puritan "stock"; one who has been most carefully trained up in the way he should go. He is quite a young man—only finished at Andover last year—fresh and unspoiled, yet very intelli-gent, entertaining and well-read. You would have been amused the other night, when he asked me to go to hear Irving; he was very awkward and embarrassed and, as you will readily understand, I liked him the better for it—"Miss Axson, would you object?—may I—ah!—I would like so much to ask—if I only *dared!*—for the pleasure of taking you, etc."

Woodrow tried to be generous about the lovely Mr. Goodrich.

Balto., Md., Nov. 13th, 1884

. . . I am delighted, my pet, that you are to see Irving and Ellen Terry. . . . I am sure that you will think, as I do, that Miss Terry is infinitely better than Irving—at least if you see them in parts anything like those in which I saw them—namely Hamlet and Ophelia. His strut is almost as execrable as his pronunciation. She is beyond comparison the finest actress I ever saw. Ah, what would I not give to see her *with you!* I envy Mr. Goodrich *with all my heart!* Wouldn't *you* rather go with me than with him? . . .

Some things in New York, however, shocked the young lady from Georgia:

New York [undated]

. . . By the way, what do you know about the "Society for Ethical Culture" and Felix Adler? Mr. Brush [a well-known artist then teaching at her art school] belongs to it and so does a pretty *young* girl in our class. It is said that they don't believe in God or even in the immortality of the soul. What a terrible faith—or no faith!—and the idea of a young *woman* adopting it!

I suppose there never was a man more dependent than I am upon love and sympathy, more devoted to home and home-life; and, my darling, my heart is filled to overflowing with gratitude and gladness because of the assurance that it now has a new love to lean upon —

Mr. Goodrich, Ellen wrote, had given her a copy of a new poem which had made a great hit—*Rubáiyát*, by Omar Khayyám, with illustrations by Elihu Vedder.

> New York, Nov. 18, 1884
>
> . . . I was wild to see it, for I have read and heard of nothing else, it seems to me, for weeks past. . . . Mr. Goodrich has been trying to obtain possession of it for some time; he brought it up and read it to me. . . . I really believe that Vedder has more genius than any other American artist; he is not merely a great workman, like so many French artists, but he is equally great on the intellectual and imaginative sides. It seems a pity, does it not, that such noble work should be expended on such a heathenish poem . . .

As for the stern young Presbyterian, he approved neither of the poem nor of the way in which Ellen had become acquainted with it.

Bryn Mawr College, which had just been founded, was interested in Woodrow Wilson as a teacher, and he was excited at the prospect of a job that would make it possible for him to marry Ellen. She, however, had misgivings:

> New York, Nov. 28/84
>
> My darling Woodrow,
>
> . . . Can you bring yourself to feel thoroughly in sympathy with that kind of thing—with the *tendencies* and *influences* of such an institution? Can you, with all your heart, cooperate with the strong-minded person who conducts it?—The *"Dean!"* how ridiculous! . . . Seriously, dear, I fear you would find it very unpleasant to serve, as it were, under a *woman!* It seems so unnatural, so jarring to one's sense of the fitness of things—so absurd too.
>
> I may be very silly to say so, but it seems to me that it is rather beneath *you* to teach in a "female college. . . ."

Woodrow was disappointed by this "earnest protest," and wrote to persuade her. He would, he assured her, "not be under a woman"; there was a male president, and several other men were on the faculty. So Ellen consented, and after some negotiations about salary—finally settled at $1,500 a year—he accepted the Bryn Mawr appointment, to begin in September, 1885.

Meanwhile, in New York, Mr. Goodrich was becoming too attentive to Ellen for Woodrow's peace of mind. He added a rather stern postscript to a letter dated December 18, 1884:

> P.S. I had meant to say something about Mr. Goodrich, in answer to your letter of this morning; and though it *is* very late, I will even now add a few words while the matter is on my mind. You were quite right in your forecast of my opinion on the subject of his attentions to you. I do *not* believe in the possibility of the "platonic schedule" *at all.* Of course I have *perfect* faith in your discreetness; but you must remember that he is in ignorance of your engagement, and that not the broadest hints conceivable can make him "understand" so long as you continue to wear your ring as you have been wearing it. Not to wear it on the significant finger is in effect to *conceal* our engagement, my pet, and nobody can be expected to understand hints in the face of the testimony of his senses. Your faith in the power of the New England climate to change human nature may be well founded; but I think it would be much fairer to me if you would wear your ring as an engagement ring. I have not insisted upon this before . . . but now I trust that my darling will see fit to observe my wishes in the matter, if she has not done so already. . . .

So Mr. Goodrich, to his pain, was admitted to the secret that Ellen was engaged. But he begged her to let him continue to see her, and promised to "acquit her beforehand of any painful consequences to him." Would Woodrow mind if she still saw him once in awhile? He minded—so much that on the day he heard from Bryn Mawr's board of trustees, he wrote five pages of protest before telling her the good news, relenting only so far as to say that he would not object to her accepting Mr. Goodrich's escort to church. "Though I shall pity him and fear that he won't derive much benefit from the church services," he added with uncharacteristic sarcasm.

Now their letters were full of plans. But Ellen Axson, artist and lover of poetry, was, at the same time, an exceedingly sensible and practical woman. She had given her consent to the Bryn Mawr appointment, because she could not bear to disappoint Woodrow, but when she sat down to examine facts and figures, she was worried. Would it not be better, she asked, to put off their marriage for another year, so that Woodrow could save for the high cost of living at Bryn Mawr? The letter he wrote in reply may not have lessened her anxiety, but it stopped any further objections.

> Balto., Jan'y 22, 1885
>
> . . . How does the case stand, then, with me? If I am to spend another year without you, it will be simple prudence to decline the Bryn Mawr offer and spend that year *here.* I

would only break myself down by undertaking such a situation alone. Pecuniary anxieties, should I be weak enough to yield dominion to them, could not torment me half as much as the double burden of novel responsibilities and loneliness. . . .

Take counsel of your *heart*, darling, not of your fears. And above all have no fears for *me!* . . . Have you so little faith in love that you think the inconveniences of imperative economy, which can have in it no actual want, enough to outweigh it with me? . . .

Ellen promised to marry him in June, and he could hardly believe it:

Balto., Sabbath afternoon
Jan'y 25, 1885

. . . The crowning, the most precious sentence in this sweet note [is] "So it must be as you wish." As I wish! *Can* it be true that I am to have, as my heart's most inestimable treasure, the loving wife for whom my life has so long waited? . . . Are you really to be my bride, my life-long sweetheart, the joy and pride of my manhood, and, if God will, the comfort and strength of my old age? Yes, you have promised! And I? What will I give in return? There is very little that I can give—except love. That is much—and you shall be rich in that. . . . If love can make a true husband, I will be one to my darling . . .

A day came when Woodrow's worldly wisdom was confirmed. Poor Mr. Goodrich, unable to control his emotions, proposed to Ellen. She told him sternly that he could never see her again, and described his reaction in a letter to Woodrow, whose indignant response arrived by the next mail.

Balto., Sabbath afternoon
Feb'y 8, 1885

. . . So Mr. G. sought his fate, did he? My brave, true little sweetheart! You have acted just as I would have you act. But what shall I say for him? If he pleaded and protested, and thought himself unjustly treated, I don't wonder that you saw how weak and unmanly the whole thing was on his part! Why, Eileen, I can't conceive of a *man's* making it *necessary* that you should have a "scene" with him. . . . He is either a fool or a knave; but I have no inclination to abuse him. I can only pity and despise a man who hasn't the manliness to see that he *owes* it to you to *anticipate* your wish to have nothing more to do with him; and I cannot sufficiently rejoice that you are finally rid of the attentions of a man whose lack of true gentlemanly instinct must have exposed you to repeated mortification. I sincerely hope that he *will* leave the house. . . .

From some of her New York acquaintances Ellen heard disturbing talk about "a woman's right to live her own life," and Woodrow was moved to vehement comment:

Balto., March 1, 1885

. . . I don't wonder that you can have no sympathy with that false talk . . . The family relation is at the foundation of society, . . . and the women who think that marriage destroys identity and is not the essential condition of the performance of their *proper* duties—if they think so *naturally* and not through disappointment—are the *only* women whom God has intended for old maids. . . . Women *have* a right to live their own lives. They have mental and moral gifts of a sort and of a perfection that men lack: but they have not the *same* gifts that men have. Their life must *supplement* man's life; and it cannot supplement man's life without being in closest wifely communion with it. This is not putting their lives in a position *subordinate* to the position allotted to men. The colours of the spectrum supplement each other, but without *all* of them we should not have the full splendour of the sun.

As June drew nearer, both of the lovers had last flickers of misgiving about their adequacy.

New York, April 3, 1885

. . . I have yet to learn whether the most perfect love, the tenderest service, the most passionate loyalty can make me, without certain qualities which love cannot give, such a wife as yours should be. But I know that, notwithstanding the demand is so much greater, I will be a better wife to you than I could ever have been to a small man, because no other but yourself could have so stirred my nature to its utmost depths, could have inspired me with such passionate longing toward my own ideal of womanhood . . .

Balto., April 5, 1885

. . . It may shock you—it ought to . . . to learn that I have a reputation (?) amongst most of my kin and certain of my friends for being irrepressible, in select circles, as a maker of grotesque addresses from the precarious elevation of chair seats, as a wearer of all varieties of comic grimaces, as a simulator of sundry unnatural burlesque styles of voice and speech, as a lover of farces, even as a dancer of the "can-can"! . . . But you'll find out soon enough what an overgrown boy you have taken as your "lord and master (?)"

New York, April 5, 1885

. . . But query!—if you know a woman so well that you are sure beforehand what she is going to say, or what she would *like* to say on any given subject, what special interest do you find in hearing her say it? Why isn't she an unmitigated bore? . . . I am inclined to think it would be hard to find any way to ward off that danger from a purely intellectual marriage. . . . If one married a Macaulay simply to hear him *talk,* one would grow tired of it in the course of years, if one didn't exhaust his resources. The novelty would wear off and the flashes of silence would be like balm to the suffering. But I know *now* that a true man and woman never weary of true love and sympathy. It is a possession which time doesn't cheapen. I remember when such questions as those I asked you above seemed to me among the greatest difficulties in the way of marriage. What *do* they talk about! I should think they would wear each other out or suffer from a most embarrassing dearth of remarks! What a foolish school-girl's idea it seems to me now! As if marriage were like an evening call where long pauses are awkward and must be avoided at any cost. . . . A never-ending evening-call!—*horrible!* . . .

Ellen had set the month for their wedding, but not, in spite of Woodrow's urging, the date. Now, at the end of a long love letter, she mentioned an approximate date, and he wrote, joyfully,

Balto., April 18, 1885

. . . Somehow it seems to me that the sun shines brighter today than it ever did before. For does not this precious letter close with one of those "By the ways" which often serve my lady to introduce the most important things she says? . . . Do you think, Miss, to escape in that way the embarrassment of fixing a particular day? To say "any day between the 24th and the 31st of June" means that we will be married on the 24th; for I shall certainly take the earliest date you offer. . . .

But it was not so simple as he supposed to fix a date for the wedding. A bride must have a trousseau, and Ellen's would take more time than usual to assemble for she had been in mourning ever since her father's death and needed an entirely new wardrobe. And, because she could not afford to buy it, she planned to make all her dresses herself when she went back to Savannah. But she had paid her tuition fees at the Art Students' League in advance until June, and she was appalled at the thought of spending money and getting nothing for it.

New York, April 19, 1885

. . . Being a man it is probable that you think three weeks more than time enough for *anything!* Perhaps I should make some concession to masculine ignorance and explain more fully. There is a great deal of sewing which I *must* do. I can't afford to have it all done for me. Here in New York the material for an inexpensive dress costs just *half* as much as the making of said dress, and in Savannah it is almost as bad. It is positively ruinous to "put out" anything but a handsome dress. So you can see my predicament—one must have some time to prepare even the most modest trousseau. . . .

To her great amusement, Woodrow had something to say about her trousseau.

Balto., April 21, 1885

. . . Don't it take less time and trouble, darling, to make straight skirts with perpendicular pleats, or like devices, and bodies of the same style, than to make flounced skirts with skewed over-skirts (you must let me use my own terms, however untechnical) and bodies with stiff necks? You know, as I confided in you when we were only friends that I have very decided tastes in ladies' dress (else I would not dare to venture into this department of inquiry where I don't know the language.) . . . I know that for some reason the close-fitting, high-necked body of your black silk dress is not at all becoming to you. . . . Is it because you are best suited by square yokes, open necks, simple pleated skirts, and—but dear me! I must get out of this just as soon as I can. What temerity! . . .

Ellen wrote, after reading this letter:

New York, April 22, 1885

. . . Would your feelings be deeply hurt, if you knew how I have been laughing over it? You have Bible authority for not liking "stiff-necked" people but what *is* a stiff-necked "body"? . . . You didn't tell me what sort of hats you like! Pray write full descriptions of them! You do it *so* well! It will afford me such exquisite delight to read it. Really I think it is *very* nice in you, dear, to take an interest in such things, and since I find you have such decided opinions about them, I am more than anxious to have them. All suggestions thankfully received! Do you like little bonnets tied under the chin or broad-brimmed hats or "turbans" or "pokes"? And perhaps I had better take your opinion on the colour question. . . .

While she painted and shopped, Ellen began to worry about those odd women at Bryn Mawr who had taken up "higher education." They would probably be condescending because she did not know as much as they. When Woodrow sent her Bryn Mawr's first catalogue, she wrote:

New York, April 26, 1885

. . . Truly they have a masculine standard "sure enough." Oh dear me! What a little goose I am! This brings it home to me afresh. I think I had better go to school there—only I couldn't get in. . . .

Balto., April 27, 1885

. . . Sweetheart, I shall agree with you that you *are* a little goose to bemoan the fact that you don't know as much as the Bryn Mawr girls are expected to know! What do you think of *my* case? I am to be one of their instructors, and yet I not only could not pass the entrance examinations, without special preparation, but could not even be an advanced student, much less a Fellow in my own department—because I can't read German at sight! But that by no means indicates that I am not infinitely better educated than my pupils will be. Both you and I have what is immeasurably better than the *information* which is all that would be needed for passing Bryn Mawr, or any other college examinations! We have the power to *think*, to *use* information. For my part I want to carry as little *information* in my head as possible. . . . It is enough if I know where to find it; for corroboration, for illustration, etc.

The day came when Ellen and Woodrow wrote to each other for the last time, or so they hoped and believed. They were sure that they would never be separated after their marriage, never again have to depend on words to express their love. Each tried to capture the essence of the moment. From his sister's house at Columbia, South Carolina, Woodrow wrote on June 21:

My own darling,

It seems altogether too good to be true that our bondage to pen and paper is at last at an end! . . . This letter will reach you on Monday, and on Tuesday I shall go to my darling, to *carry* the words of love with which my heart is so full . . . to consecrate to her my life, that it may be spent in making perfect the fulfilment of all the sweet promises in which our love for each other is so rich. . . . I feel as if this last love-*message* were in some sort sacred. My deepest, strongest desire in marrying you, darling, is to make you happy, and I would put into this letter some word of love which would seem to your heart a sort of sweet preface to the book of love which we are about to open together, to read new secrets of sympathy and companionship. I would have you catch a glimpse of my purpose for the future and of the joy which that future contains *for me,* of the gratitude I feel for your priceless gift of love, and of the infinite love and tenderness which is the gift of my whole heart to you. . . . Good bye, then, sweetheart, till Tuesday. God willing, I shall come to claim a part of your welcome then: . . . the next time that I hold you to my heart will be the happiest moment of all my life, and the delicious prelude to still happier hours when you will be constantly at my side to tell me of the love that is more than life to me. Darling, once more I pledge you all my love and honour. I *love* you. With all my heart, in all my thoughts and hopes and purposes I am

Your own,
Woodrow

Savannah, June 20/85

And can it really be possible, my darling, that this is my *last* letter to you? . . . How strange it seems to think that we will have no more need of letters!—how strangely sweet! And yet the letters have been *so* dear to me, and will always be my carefully guarded treasure even when I have you too. They have made so large a part of my life for so long that I daresay I will still be listening and watching for the postman many a time when I am even at your side.

. . . I would that I could tell you in this last letter something more than I have ever told before of what *love* means for me. But there are few places in my heart which I have

not opened to you, dearest; I have shown you my heart of hearts. . . . You know as well as you *can* know, before the years have brought their proof, how absolutely I am yours; you know the depth and tenderness and fervour of my love . . . Darling, my *faith* in you is a part of my *love* for you; the one no less than the other has become the ruling *passion* as well as the controlling principle of my life. Thank God that the man I love is one who will permit me to obey His marriage law. I am to promise next week to *reverence* you. How many of the young men I have known do you suppose it would be *possible* to reverence! But you will be in very truth my head—my being, not only because *I* will it but because *God* wills it, because He made you so to be.

. . . And now, good-bye, my dear one, till Tuesday. I love you, darling, as much as you would have me love you. . . . Perhaps you have not yet sounded all the depths of my heart, yet to the very bottom it *is all yours* and I am for life —and death,

Your own Eileen

What a sweet preparation we have had for our wedding day! How precious the experience of these months of our engagement has been!

On the twenty-fourth of June, in 1885, Ellen Louise Axson and Woodrow Wilson were married. It was an evening wedding in the parlor of the manse, next door to the Independent Presbyterian Church in Savannah. Dr. I. S. K. Axson, the bride's grandfather, and Dr. Joseph R. Wilson, the bridegroom's father, stood side by side and shared the reading of the marriage ceremony. The parlor, with its high ceiling and dignified furnishings, was large but barely large enough to hold all the relatives. Ellen wore the traditional white veil and a simple white dress which she herself had made. The groom wore his dress-suit. They looked so happy that all the women cried.

Their honeymoon was two idyllic weeks at Arden Park, in the mountains of North Carolina. In September, they settled down contentedly in a house on the edge of the college campus at Bryn Mawr, Pennsylvania—the beginning of a marriage that would last happily until Ellen's death at the White House in 1914, and that would play a vital part in projecting Woodrow Wilson onto the great stage of world history. Through all those formative years her enduring love was indeed, for him, "a priceless gift."

The Dark World of ✐ David Gilmour Blythe

CONTINUED FROM PAGE 20

on the road and awakened to realize that his horse had thrown him into a ditch on top of the produce he had collected in exchange for shoes: eggs, butter, an outraged turkey gobbler. That Sunday, the boarders found on the parlor mantel a drawing of the scene. As laughter rocked through the village, Blythe achieved, at the age of thirty-one, friends and a home.

It seemed to him now, after so much wandering in search of he knew not what, that dear companions were what he had always most desired. From his studio, known as "the rat's nest," Blythe issued to mix liquor, jokes, and art. As a good fellow, he was considered a greater painter than Sir Joshua Reynolds—with whose work Uniontown was far from familiar. According to local anecdote, a judge (he must have been very nearsighted) bowed to one of Blythe's portraits thinking it the actual man, and a lady (she must have been desperate for attention) almost fainted before the same likeness, exclaiming that she had seen a ghost.

With an adze as his basic tool and a tiny engraving for a model, Blythe carved from poplar a statue of Lafayette that stood eight feet two inches in its shoes. The unveiling of this wonder was one of Uniontown's proudest days. Waving a perpetually refilled glass, the sculptor acknowledged the plaudits of the citizens, while beside him the wooden patriot towered motionless, one hand in the pocket of an immense frock coat and the other grasping the high hat which a tinsmith had fashioned. While the militia fired volleys in salute, the image was hoisted to its position topping the dome of the Fayette County Courthouse. Now, so Blythe rhymed in one of the occasional verses he wrote, every eye could see against the firmament

> . . . the chaste outline of one
> Who was the friend of Washington.

As a balance to male conviviality, Blythe frequented the drawing rooms of young ladies who were "all virgin purity," adorned, so he wrote in their albums, with flowers plucked in Eden. One girl especially seemed to be "from that land where sin and suffering cease." She became his wife. Now, so he exulted, "hope is lined with velvet."

Within less than a year his wife died, and he cried out:

> 'Tis past! There was but one unbroken link
> That held me trembling on the brink;
> But that is gone,
> And now I sink!
> Alone! Alone!

He sought other girls, but now women seemed less a gift of purity than a temptation to evil. And as he drank ever more heavily, he became increasingly bellicose. Still remembered on both banks of the Monongahela was his personal war with neighboring Greene County, which lusted after a courthouse statue as elegant as his Lafayette. Delegates called on him to order one of General Nathanael Greene, but when Blythe asked $300, they replied that they had not intended to give him the whole county and that they had a carpenter at home who would do it for half the price. Blythe thereupon published in Uniontown newspapers poems calling Greene County "a sow grown fat with buttermilk and meal," and commenting on the bedbugs and the crowding of its taverns. Since one of the taverns maintained sixteen beds in a room nicknamed "the prairie," Blythe had touched on a sore spot. When a poet in a Greene County paper accused him of being too drunken to be worth listening to, Blythe dismissed his attacker as "the son of an insolvent rat." (This brought into the fray another Greene County champion whom Blythe characterized as "a growling, whining hound.") An effort was made to lure the artist over the border so that Greene County could ride him on a rail, but in the taverns of Uniontown he was more than ever a hero.

Blythe now established a partnership with two boon companions: they would pay the costs, and he would paint a series of huge views showing the landscape and historical events of western Pennsylvania. Sewed together to form a canvas strip seven feet high and three hundred feet long that could be passed from one roller to another, this became one of those precursors of the movies, a panorama. The narrator who lectured on the passing pictures to audiences both skeptical and gay had to keep his wits about him. Thus, when a backwoodsman rose to ask how a deer with tremendous antlers had got them through the thicket from which he was shown emerging, the speaker answered crushingly, "That's his business!"

As the partners toured with the panorama—they got as far as Baltimore—Blythe became unmanageable. He insisted on doing the lecture himself, but got too drunk to be understood. His associates, recently his dearest Uniontown friends, finally abandoned him. The panorama was seized for debt. In anger and bitterness, Blythe banished himself from Uniontown. He no longer had a home.

In a poem written about this time, Blythe could now describe himself:

Out from the cold, blank emptiness
Of a drunkard's home slowly and hushed as
A gnome-shade vomited from the green pestilent
Stomach of a sepulcher, comes forth a thing
The supplicant tongue of charity might
Hesitate to call a man, . . .
His eyes like angry, ill-closed, half-healed
Wounds, physicianless.

Returning to his old trade of itinerant portrait painting, Blythe wandered for five years, no one knows exactly where, "becoming," as he wrote, "half demented trying to find some place . . . where man and man can live together in unity." But it was not such an idyllic spot that his spirit really craved. As long as he had kept his peace with the world around him, he had produced only trivial art. Now that he had given in to a personal despair like that of a fellow alcoholic, Edgar Allan Poe, his portraits began to take on force—though unlike Poe (whose poems he sometimes imitated), Blythe was not a visionary able to give substance to altogether-subjective terrors. He needed exterior horrors to echo his interior moods, and he found them at last in the monstrous growing pains of industrialism.

Every time Blythe had visited Pittsburgh the air had been fouler, the sky sootier by day and more lurid with strange flames by night, the water front noisier and dirtier, the streets more full of grand carriages and beggars, of foreign tongues and dark faces, bewildered, angry, and confused. In 1856 he settled there, and, as he watched, the panic of 1857 slowed the whirling dance of death into a ghastly pavan. When the mills shut down, the skies cleared, and the pounding abated, but only to make more sharp the sight and sound of individual human anguish.

Through this noisome world walked the tall painter, often unsteadily, his unkempt red beard protruding from under a tepeelike buffalo-fur hat that half extinguished his face. A suit he had made himself flapped on his emaciated form. When an event or person interested him, he would lean his chin on his cane and stare silently, oblivious of any embarrassment he was causing, for minutes at a time. If, after he had dashed down on canvas what he had seen, the resulting picture offended, he merely expressed amusement at his victims' "writhings."

Thus, when past forty, Blythe began the creation on which his reputation rests: angry scenes of Pittsburgh life. In the haunts of the respectable—churches, business offices, and courthouses (he was no longer admitted to drawing rooms)—and in the respectable themselves he found only pompous hypocrisy, but for beggars, drunkards, and thieves his heart warmed with pity. It was the pity of the surgeon—or the psychiatrist—who lays cankers bare.

Again and again, Blythe struck harsh notes unsounded at that time in American painting (for parallels one would have to look to some of his French contemporaries—of whom he undoubtedly knew nothing). Although the Civil War impended, American art still reflected almost exclusively the kind of optimism that Susan Blythe had felt as she had floated down the Ohio. Grounding their attitudes on three centuries of national growth and well-being, recognizing America as still primarily a rural land, figure painters hymned with William Sidney Mount the joys of eastern farm life; with George Caleb Bingham, the masculine amusements of the rivers and hamlets of the West. It was Blythe's personal maladjustments that made him seek what was ugly in a smiling world, made him express angers, depressions, and sadisms similar to those which seventy years of historical tragedy—the Revolution, Napoleonic defeats, tyrannies, the abortive uprisings of 1830 and 1848—had implanted in French art.

Blythe's concern with cities, their law courts and their tatterdemalions, was like that of the Parisian cartoonist-painter Daumier. Blythe could show that fascination with violence and physical suffering that characterized so much Gallic figure painting. And when he depicted rural life, he substituted for the prosperous farmers Americans were accustomed to see in paintings, peasants as disfigured by labor and brutalized by poverty as those by Millet which were at the moment shocking the French Salon.

It was not Blythe, an eccentric hardly known outside western Pennsylvania, but Poe, the inspirer of many younger French writers, who brought American neuroses to bear on European creation. Yet Blythe's attitudes pointed further into the future than Poe's. Unlike Poe, he found in sickness and misery nothing heroic: they merely caused pain and despair. In this he anticipated the defeatism of much twentieth-century European art. His repellent, bewildered, helplessly suffering protagonists would be at home in the pages of Kafka.

Since Blythe could, when he wished, draw realistically, it was not incompetence that produced his often hideous distortions of the human figure. He showed the run of mankind as squat, wrapped in unlovely flesh, bloated and stupefied with unhealthy blood. Then there were the supermen, the oppressors. Like the brute who wields the whip in Blythe's masterpiece, *Pittsburgh Horse Market,* they have been thinned down by their own demoniac energy into virtual skeletons: no flesh seems to soften the aggressive jutting of their grinning jaws. He painted trials in which the lank, evil prosecutor is all-persuasive, the judge and jury boobies, and the victim too deep in the degradation of the human lot to do more than stare hopelessly, while occupying his hands in the idiotic whittling of a stick.*

The power of Blythe's conceptions was greater than his success in giving them expression—and in this he was inferior to Poe. Surely he never had a single day's artistic instruction, and in his whole lifetime hardly saw a painting worthy of the name. That his sources were mainly black-and-white engravings may have accounted for his weakness in color, which tended toward an all-pervasive yellow-brown. Not that he particularly cared. He was too eager to achieve ends to give much thought to means. For his flights, he relied on the erratic wings of his often-alcoholic inspiration. As a result, his output was shockingly uneven, and his best canvases contain, beside brilliant strokes, flaws of conception and execution.

Blythe seems to have cultivated confusion in his pictures much as he did in his own life. Having withdrawn from society—"he seldom," an admirer recorded, "associated with anyone"—he liked to hide clues and symbols necessary for comprehension of his pictures in dark corners where the eye must grope for them. Thus wilfully casting obscurities between his art and his audience, Blythe was again strangely modern.

His main concession to the genre style of his own time was to present his unhappy visions as humor. Sometimes he seems to have been genuinely amused, as in his series lampooning the ballooning crinolines in which women enveloped their lower parts, but usually his comic action is on the order of the episode he includes so often in his more crowded pictures that it almost becomes a trademark: a little boy picking a prosperous pocket.

Although later historians of Pittsburgh have thought it best to suppress Blythe's testimony, the pictures, which often mocked well-known characters, so suited his own rough times that when they were exhibited in the window of an art store, laughing crowds blocked the streets. The excitement was increased by reports— which electrified that money-grubbing society—that the artist disdained money. It was said that if rich patrons found their way up the filthy stairs to his attic room, Blythe would hardly let them sit down. Should they offer to buy a picture, he would fly into a rage. He hated to relinquish a picture to his dealer, and then he never asked whether it had been sold. The dealer, who easily disposed of his work, left orders that Blythe be given any money he asked for. He could, one Pittsburgher would whisper incredulously to another, draw *a thousand dollars;* but he never asked for more than five.

When the Civil War broke out, Blythe shambled into the field after a local regiment, wandering as a civilian from campfire to campfire and occasionally being arrested because of "his queer appearance and apparently aimless actions." But he did have an aim. He wished to witness a battle: "I think such a scene would be worth almost a life," he wrote. Although the regiment and Blythe returned without meeting the enemy, the disasters of war so appealed to his aesthetic sense that for once he was able to paint things he had not actually seen. His *Libby Prison* (see AMERICAN HERITAGE, August, 1959, page 4), showing Union soldiers suffering and dying in captivity, is one of the most gruesome of American paintings. By some psychological twist, when he imagined soldiers marching toward death at Gettysburg, he put them in a landscape that strikes, for the only time in his entire career, a tender, lyrical note.

The carnage stirred in Blythe old ambitions for fruitful contact with the world. He would paint a panorama summarizing the Civil War; he would lecture, as the rollers turned, to enraptured crowds; waves of applause would carry him across the Alleghenies to New York; across the ocean to London, to Paris, to all the great cities he had never seen. He would be at last the success his mother had wanted him to be! But although he was not yet fifty, he no longer had the strength to fill in the huge scene-painter's canvases, nor the will. He would rather drink and mourn that he had always been "a mark for destiny, or fate, or chance (no matter what) to fling their poisoned arrows at." It was on May 15, 1865, that David Gilmour Blythe died of the aggravated effects of extreme alcoholism.

---

* In 1856, writing a letter in the form of a poem to an old Uniontown friend, Blythe had this to say about the courts of law in his day:

> Our courts with few exceptions
> Are fit subjects for . . . objections.
> Public opinion first, Blackstone second,
> Now-a-days. And then our juries,
> Oh, if there's such a thing as "furies"
> Why don't they pitch in? Curious,
> Just imagine twelve ignoramuses
> With flat heads . . .
> Sitting in judgement on an intricate
> Case of law. Beautiful, isn't it?

James Thomas Flexner is the author of many books, the latest of which is That Wilder Image: The Painting of America's Native School from Thomas Cole to Winslow Homer, *to be published by Little, Brown. He contributed an article on William Sidney Mount to our August, 1960, issue.*

For further reading: The Life and Work of David G. Blythe, *by Dorothy Miller (University of Pittsburgh, 1950).*

BROTHERS REUNITED

Sirs:

When an historical mystery is exposed to your readers, it is apparently likely to be resolved. In your April, 1961, issue, you published an article entitled "Brother Against Brother" based on the letters I furnished you between two of my ancestors. My great-grandfather, John C. Pratt of Boston, was writing his brother, Jabez David Pratt of Baltimore. As the Civil War drew on . . . the brothers argued over the increasingly bitter issues, the correspondence angrily broke off, and you noted: "So the story ends. . . . whether the two men adjusted their differences and struck hands once more as brothers . . . this, like so many other questions arising out of the Civil War, goes off into mystery."

Since publication, however, I have received a number of letters. The first came from Mr. Owen A. Sheffield of Hackensack, New Jersey, who . . . is compiling a history of Dun & Bradstreet . . . He has kindly sent me copies of letters taken from facsimiles of the copying-press book of R. G. Dun, who in 1865 bought out J. D. Pratt & Co. completely. . . .

On February 18, 1865, Dun wrote to Jabez Pratt, "Your brother called on me today and read over the enclosed document and seemed to think it was all right." Since, in an earlier letter, dated February 3, 1865, Dun had written to Jabez: "I . . . regret exceedingly to hear of your continued declining health," it is reasonable to believe that Jabez, unable to continue the management of his business, had already sought the advice of his brother John. . . . Dated [March 21, 1865] there follows a letter from Dun to John C. Pratt of Boston [which] would seem to indicate that John C. Pratt may have been executor for his brother's estate and fortifies Mr. Sheffield's opinion that, in the closing days of his life, Jabez had turned to brother John.

This interpretation has been given further credence by two additional letters from readers of AMERICAN HERITAGE. The first of these came from Mrs. Louis Mortimer Pratt, Jr., of Boston who wrote: "My husband is Jabez Pratt's only grandson . . . he remembers several of John C. Pratt's children and wonders which one was your grandfather." The second letter, from Mrs. Gertrude Pratt Vance of Lemoyne, Pennsylvania, granddaughter of John C. Pratt by a second marriage, tells more. Mrs. Vance . . . informs me that: "Louis Mortimer Pratt's father, Louis Mortimer Pratt, Sr., was the youngest son of Jabez Pratt—born after his father's death. He was brought up by his uncle, John C. Pratt." According to another letter from Mrs. Pratt, Jabez's wife, Lucy, moved north after his death and died soon after the birth of their youngest child. Although it is not clear whether the brothers ever again met face to face, the knowledge that the son of Jabez lived and grew to manhood among the children of John is evidence enough that bitterness was buried and the ties of family reaffirmed.

Elizabeth Pratt Holthusen
New York City

A HERO HYMNED

Likewise, when an historical generalization is made in our pages, it is likely to be challenged. In our December, 1961, issue Virginius Dabney described "Jack Jouett's Ride," the heroic all-night gallop in 1781 whereby a devoted Virginia patriot saved Thomas Jefferson and other leaders of the rebel cause from capture by the British. The flip subhead we supplied under Mr. Dabney's title read: "His feat was more daring than Paul Revere's, but Virginia's hero had, alas, no Longfellow."

To Mr. Dabney's office at the Richmond *Times-Dispatch* came the following letter:

"In your search for a poem, did you ever come across one by Mrs. Julia Johnson Davis, late of Norfolk? It was published about ten or twelve years ago in a collection of hers called *The Garnet Ring*. It begins like this:

The blue Virginia hills were dark,
The good folk all were sleeping,
For with the British far away
What watch should they be keeping?

The poem ends:

And Tarlton galloping down the road
With his troopers swinging after,
Heard, clearer than a thrush's note,
A burst of mocking laughter.

There are some twenty stanzas in between. It sticks very close to the facts as you gave them . . . We heard that Mrs. Davis died this past December. . . .

Sister Johanna, O.S.A.
Convent of St. Anne, Kingston, New York"

At least four other readers—Major R. A. Lambie, U.S.A.F., of Scott Air Force Base in Illinois; Hugh R. Rogers of Trenton, New Jersey; Mrs. C. D. Bruce of Santa Anna, Texas; and Barbara Wade, age fifteen, of Pensacola, Florida—were inspired by the challenge to compose Jouett odes of their own, and Maurice E. Peloubet of New York City sent along a Jouett ballad he had written and distributed to friends as a Christmas greeting in 1951. From Mrs. Julia Brett Rouzee of Manhasset, Long Island, came an excellent poem, too long for our space, by her father, Homer Brett, formerly a consul-general in the U.S. Foreign Service. Entitled "Jack Jouett's Ride," it was published in a private edition of Mr. Brett's poems in 1953. Finally, Charles W. Starcher of Charleston, West Virginia, recalled reading a poem about Jouett's exploit in the seventh grade. Further research on his part unearthed "A Hawk from Cuckoo Tavern," by Lawrence Lee, which appeared in a 1933 Lippincott anthology entitled *Great Americans, As Seen by the Poets*, edited by Burton Stevenson. It even has a Longfellow-like ring to it:

Listen, Americans! Never forget
The glorious deed of Jack Jouett!
From Cuckoo Tavern a perilous ride
Across the Virginia countryside. . . .

Safe are Jefferson, Henry and Lee,
Safe is Jouett, racing free.
Saved the Assembly at Charlottesville
By the noble horse and Jouett's will. . . .

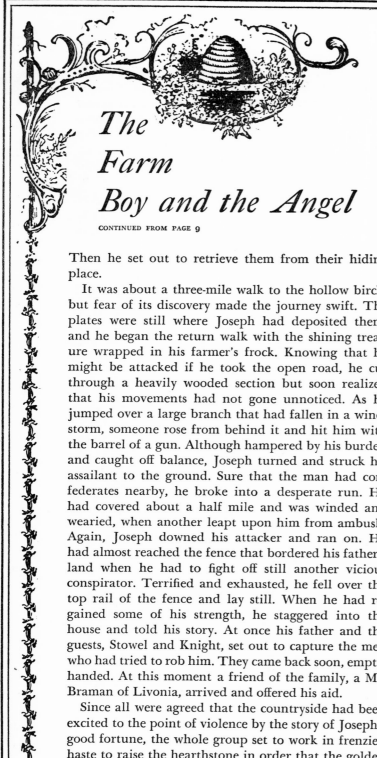

The Farm Boy and the Angel

CONTINUED FROM PAGE 9

Then he set out to retrieve them from their hiding place.

It was about a three-mile walk to the hollow birch, but fear of its discovery made the journey swift. The plates were still where Joseph had deposited them, and he began the return walk with the shining treasure wrapped in his farmer's frock. Knowing that he might be attacked if he took the open road, he cut through a heavily wooded section but soon realized that his movements had not gone unnoticed. As he jumped over a large branch that had fallen in a windstorm, someone rose from behind it and hit him with the barrel of a gun. Although hampered by his burden and caught off balance, Joseph turned and struck his assailant to the ground. Sure that the man had confederates nearby, he broke into a desperate run. He had covered about a half mile and was winded and wearied, when another leapt upon him from ambush. Again, Joseph downed his attacker and ran on. He had almost reached the fence that bordered his father's land when he had to fight off still another vicious conspirator. Terrified and exhausted, he fell over the top rail of the fence and lay still. When he had regained some of his strength, he staggered into the house and told his story. At once his father and the guests, Stowel and Knight, set out to capture the men who had tried to rob him. They came back soon, empty-handed. At this moment a friend of the family, a Mr. Braman of Livonia, arrived and offered his aid.

Since all were agreed that the countryside had been excited to the point of violence by the story of Joseph's good fortune, the whole group set to work in frenzied haste to raise the hearthstone in order that the golden book, the breastplate, and the diamond spectacles might be secreted beneath it. They had hardly completed the job when an armed and angry mob appeared before the house. Here, Joseph adopted a stratagem that he had learned from the tales of his

The beehive border is from an early edition of the Book of Mormon; the honeybee is a symbol of fruitful industry.

mother's father, Solomon Mack, who had fought in the American Revolution. Opening all the doors of the little house, he began giving orders in a loud voice —as if he had many men to command. Then at his signal all of the besieged, even little Don Carlos, ran out as if to attack. The mob wavered—then fled.

Realizing that their enemies would soon return in greater force, the Smiths and their friends considered how best to outwit them. They raised the hearthstone once more and took from under it the box which held the treasures. Joseph lifted them out, covered them with cloths, and carried them to a cooper's shop across the way. Under a pile of flax in the loft he hid his precious burden. Then he nailed the cover back on the box, tore up the floor of the shop, set the empty receptacle below, and replaced the floor boards.

When darkness came, the mob returned. This time there was no stopping them. They swarmed about the Smith house, searching every inch of ground but finding nothing. By this time they had lost faith in the imported conjurer and were placing their confidence in Willard Chase's sister, who, having found a stone of a strange green color, claimed that by looking into it she could see "where Joe Smith kept his Bible hid." Apparently her assumed clairvoyance had led to the box, for in the morning the Smiths found the floor of the cooper shop once more torn up and the wooden chest splintered into many pieces. The treasures were safe in the loft beneath the flax.

This is the "origin story" of the religious sect known formally as the Church of Jesus Christ of Latter-day Saints, informally as "the Mormons." All conversion to the Mormon creed begins with the acceptance of this miracle-fraught narrative. John Henry Evans, Mormon historian, who has written one of the most objective and thoughtful biographies of Joseph Smith, delivers plainly the accepted Mormon attitude: "Mormonism has its basis on the miraculous element in religion, or it has no foundation at all on which to stand. They are fooling themselves, whether within or without the Mormon church, who think they can accept the faith of Joseph Smith and at the same time reject the visions of Joseph Smith. No such choice is permissible. One must believe these supernormal experiences and Mormonism, or one must reject Mormonism with the visions."

When young Joseph Smith was ten years old his mother bore another son—who was romantically christened Don Carlos. The new baby was the ninth of her children, and only one, Ephraim, had died. The prospect of having to feed ten mouths moved the father to set out from his high barrens above the Connecticut River at Norwich and seek an opportunity for a better living in newly developed lands to the west. With him went a like-minded neighbor named Howard. Considerations other than unfertile soil strengthened the decision of these men, for this was 1816, ever afterward reviled as "old eighteen-hundred-and-froze-to-death." Because most of their crops froze, the Yankees called it "poverty year" or, since the only food obtainable was from the coast fisheries, "mackerel year."

From the high perch above the White River, the older Smith children and their mother with her baby could see irregular blotches on a cold sun. In early June came almost intolerable heat and, suddenly, sunspots again and snow and fierce cold that froze the new-plowed acres hard. After that, each day dawned to bright frost and dry weather. Even hot-weather birds—goldfinches and scarlet sparrows—took refuge in houses, where people could pick them up in their hands to warm their numbed bodies.

In July snow lay on the summits of the Green Mountains. The smoke of wood fires dimmed the wintry weeks of a summer that had vanished. For one hundred and twenty days there was no rain. A farmer said that when he was mowing the lower forty on the fourth of July, he had seen an antlered buck leap a stone fence and land in a snowdrift so deep he could not move before the scythe had decapitated him and provided venison for a large family.

In the midst of this long drought, unexpected hope came to the Smiths. Mr. Howard appeared at their door to tell Lucy that in western York State he and her husband had come upon the busy town of Palmyra, in which they thought they might prosper. Father Smith had sent word to the family to sell what they could not pack, pay their debts, and accompany Mr. Howard when he set out on his return.

No sooner had she told her Norwich neighbors that the family was moving west than they gathered like vultures. Knowing that the decision was final, they made ridiculously low offers for the farm possessions, and she was forced to accept them. Soon Mr. Howard was clucking to the Smith team, and the overloaded Smith buckboard was rattling along the road south.

Lucy was forty years old that summer. With her new baby at her breast and seven older children, she was leaving the mountains she had always known and making the journey to the Genesee country far across the state of New York.

The mother soon discovered that Mr. Howard, the one adult male of the expedition, was dissatisfied and sullenly unco-operative. He disciplined her children

strictly, and she quarreled with him over his treatment of young Joseph. He had decided that the older children should walk as much of the way as possible. Samuel Harrison, eight; William, five; Catherine, four; and baby Don Carlos were obviously too small to keep up with the wagon. Joseph was still recovering from an operation that had taken place two years before. Without aid of anesthetic a primitive surgeon had lanced an infection on his knee and, cutting deep below it, had scraped the bone. Afterward the boy had been sent to his uncle, Jesse Smith, who lived in Salem, Massachusetts, in the hope that salt sea air might improve his general condition, but he still limped. Howard ignored this and ordered him out of the wagon time and time again.

When the Smith caravan left the old Dutch town of Albany on the Great Western Turnpike, they were not alone. Hundreds of Yankee farmers, disheartened by the stony soil and freezing weather, had pulled up stakes and were rolling west to the fertile ground and the mild climate which they had been told they would find beside the fresh-water seas. Promise of thriving business lay in every swaying stagecoach that plunged past, in every freight wagon thundering over the deep-rutted road with the driver cracking his long whip over the eight-horse team. Peddlers' wagons—"flying stores"—jingled to a stop here and there, and the owners exhibited glittering wares and shouted their praises. Taverns along the way swarmed with loud-voiced patrons and hurrying servants.

At one of these hostelries, about twenty miles west of Utica, Lucy Smith, preparing in early morning for another day on the road, heard the excited report of her son Alvin that Mr. Howard had thrown their goods on the ground and was about to drive off with the wagon and team. She told the boy to order the driver to the barroom. He came, and they met in a noisy crowd of travelers. Lucy demanded an explanation, and Howard answered that the money she had given him for the trip had run out and he had quit.

The blood of her Scottish preacher ancestors, the spirit of her soldier-father, Solomon Mack, who had fought the French and Indians and later the British, asserted themselves. She spoke out so loudly and so sharply that the chattering men and women about her

ILLUSTRATIONS: CULVER PICTURES

Palmyra, New York, as it looked at about the time Joseph Smith lived there. He came west from Vermont as a boy and remained in the vicinity until he was grown.

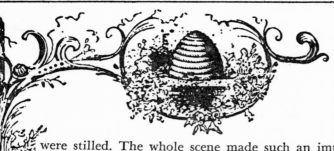

were stilled. The whole scene made such an impression upon her memory, she wrote years later, that she could recall her every word. "Gentlemen and ladies," she said, "please give your attention for a moment. Now, as sure as there is a God in heaven, that team, as well as the goods, belong to my husband, and this man intends to take them from me . . . leaving me with eight children, without the means of proceeding on my journey."

She turned to Howard: "Sir," she said, "I now forbid your touching the team or driving it one step further. You can go about your own business; I have no use for you. I shall take charge of the team myself; and hereafter attend to my own affairs."

Then she walked out to the horses and took up the reins while Howard slunk away.

The lame, unsmiling towhead would walk little now. He would ride and think, and he had more to think on than most boys on the west-rolling wagons. In his first decade, and possibly before his memory took hold, his parents had moved him from their Sharon, Vermont, farm, boulder-peppered, steep, and lonesome above the tumbling White River, to busy Tunbridge.

In that town, before his birth, his father had once set up a shop and his mother had tended it, and the two of them had risked their savings on a profitless venture—shipping to China ginseng roots, said to be in demand as revivers of sexual potency.

They found the return to Tunbridge with little Joseph disappointing and set out for nearby Royalton, which also had failed them once and now did so again. Then they tried Lebanon, New Hampshire, in the Connecticut's smiling valley. By this time Joseph was about seven and fully aware of his changing environs. For several months here the family did so well that they could afford to enter Hyrum at Moore's Academy across the river at Hanover. From this school he came home with a fever instantly communicated to his brothers and sisters. Thence came the infection on Joseph's leg and the savage operation. Once more the family moved back to Vermont and a fertile Norwich farm which kept none of its promises because of three successive crop failures, the last being in desolate 1816.

During all the peregrinations through little Yankee towns, Joseph had known two old men who had left their marks upon him. One was white-haired Grand-

father Mack, who, come a-visiting, would painfully climb down from the sidesaddle on his rib-striped mare to tell the family stories of the days when he was a hero in battles against the painted, whooping Indians, the slick and monstrous-cruel "monseers," the dim-witted British lobster-backs. When Joseph was five the old man had brought the Smiths a book in which his tales had been printed, and daughter Lucy never tired of reading them to her children.

The other old man was Grandfather Asael Smith, tall and well filled-out but of strange appearance because a burn on his neck when he was young caused him to carry his head to one side—"Crooked-neck Smith," folks called him. He, too, had fought in the War of Independence and so had his father—but he said little about it. He was a thoughtful man who had ideas and stuck to them even when the whole of Topsfield, his home town in Vermont, disagreed. He was a man to talk about a boy's behavior and his work and his thoughts about God. He was both serious and powerful but of a gentle nature, never seeking trouble, though he never avoided it either. Joseph had not seen as much of Asael Smith as he had of Solomon Mack, but Asael was not someone to forget.

Most recent of Joseph's memories and most vivid as he bounced along on the buckboard was the seaport, Salem, which he had left only a few months before his father had set out for the west. To a Vermont farm boy whose parents were almost continually on the move, this town could not have failed to provide a symbol of continuing wealth, stability, and romance.

The big many-windowed houses enhanced by neat trim and neater fences looked as if they had stood for generations, as indeed some of them had. The lovely doors that opened on Essex Street, Washington Square, and Chestnut Street offered entrance to rooms filled with elegancies that had come from far—mahoganies from the West Indies, silvers from England, porcelains from China. The families who owned them, richly dressed and dignified, walked the cobbled streets as if they knew of no world of sterile acres and mounting debts. Down by the harbor docks, where merchant-wanderers of the sea rocked at anchor and the winds freed wild odors of Canton tea, Brazilian coffee, and spices from a hundred islands, dark-visaged sailors spat and swore and embroidered narratives of their adventures. Among the Salem boys who looked and smelled and listened, there was one dark and handsome and a year older than Joseph—Nathaniel Hawthorne. This boy's father, a sea captain, had died in Surinam when his son was four. Since, at the time of Joseph's visit, Nathaniel was very lame from an injury in a ball game, the boys may have found a bond in their common affliction. Nathaniel was one day to reveal in his books the influence of his Salem surroundings upon him. That they had a lasting and significant effect on sensitive, blond Joseph as well is not to be doubted, though few of his biographers have suggested it. The town had caught his fancy, and years later he would come back to Salem still believing that priceless treasures brought from across the ocean had been concealed in some of its old houses.

And so, for a ten-year-old, Joseph was something of a sophisticate as he journeyed toward Palmyra. He had had several homes in small Vermont towns; he had known disease and had withstood almost intolerable pain; he had visited in a seaport where talk was of the world rather than a county; he had observed many an inexplicable and wondrous act of nature. As later associates, both enemies and friends, discovered, he had a kind of blotter-mind that soaked up at once such facts and impressions as interested him.

There was much along the Great Western Turnpike that would fascinate a boy of this sort. After his mother had rid herself of Howard and taken command, the Smith party passed through busy Manlius, where four turnpikes, spreading like rays from a star, crossed each other. Beyond lay Green Pond (unblinking eye of shadowed water set two hundred feet below the precipitous bluffs that were its shores), and nearby a well-digger had come upon an echoing cavern so spread beneath its grotesquely shaped ceilings that no man could say how far it extended or what might be found within it.

These sights proved to be omens, forerunners to the Smiths of stranger phenomena that they would find when they neared their journey's end. The long slopes of the York State hills began to flatten out as they approached Palmyra. The Great Western Turnpike led them neither up nor down, and the horses trotted easily on a spreading plain striped by narrow blue lakes and dotted with green pyramids. They had entered the land of the drumlins.

Few settlers thought of these greenery-covered piles of earth and rock as created in the ice age by glacial action. Their neat geometric design and their smallness suggested that they were man-made mounds, cones of earth erected by prehistoric tribes, and that they might contain precious relics of a long-forgotten era.

There is no detailed account of the Smith family's reunion with father Joseph at Palmyra. Since they were a loyal, affectionate group

it can be assumed that, though Lucy had only two pennies and a small portion of their belongings left, it was joyous. It signaled, moreover, a period of intense activity for them all. Twice as big as Norwich, Palmyra was a bustling town of over three thousand, and it anticipated a rapid and limitless expansion. Situated on the expected route of the Great Western Canal that Governor De Witt Clinton was determined to build, the town saw itself within a few years a widespread commercial port on a man-made river. Father Smith could well expect that the "cake and beer" shop that Lucy at once started would prosper. Gingerbread, boiled eggs, pies, and root beer found eager customers, particularly among children, and Lucy added for adults oilcloth table covers which she had a knack for decorating with colorful designs.

The drumlin country and its environs held wonders that fascinated its inhabitants, who had come, for the most part, from New England, a land of less startling natural phenomena. They felt now as if they had entered a ring of enchantment. At Bristol, south of Palmyra, springs brushed by a torch bubbled into blue and yellow flames. A few miles nearer, every detail of the variegated world of weeds and rocks had become part of one wide monochrome—yellowed by spattering dye from the sulphurous fountains of Clifton. Where their acres had not been cleared, the settlers gaped at towering exotics—tulip and cucumber trees—or at a hollow buttonwood in which a church elder had preached to a congregation of thirty-five. (He said reprovingly that it would have held fifteen more.) Plowmen uncovered, lying like logs in the earth, many a bulbous root—three or four feet long and six to eight inches in diameter—which looked for all the world like a nude male body. "Man-in-the-ground" they called it, and they speculated darkly on its powers. Colored stones of fantastic shapes jeweled the banks of meandering Mud Creek, and now and again among them flashed a prism of translucent selenite, which oldsters called moonstone because, they said, it waxed and waned with phases of the moon. This was a land for a boy to wander in. It stirred a sensitive mind to creative imaginings.

Lafayette, the aging hero of the Revolution, landed in New York in August, 1824, and on his triumphal tour visited upper New York State. Joseph Smith's love of pageantry may have dated from such events.

As strange as the atmosphere created by the drumlin country was the talk of the people. Only a few of the pioneers were learned, and superstition stirred the others into unchanneled reckonings. There were long-continued discussions of the ignorant farm girl, Rachel Baker, a neighbor who had amazed the countryside for two years by preaching eloquently in her sleep.

The boy Joseph Smith would come much closer to another and more powerful personality in the next few years. She, too, seemed by background and schooling completely unequipped for the work which, she assured all who would listen, had been chosen for her by God. It was her claim that in 1776 when she was Jemima Wilkinson, an unschooled maiden of eighteen, she had expired of a fever in Rhode Island. No sooner, she said, had her soul left her slim, lithe body than the "Spirit of Life from God" had inhabited it. At once she had risen from the dead proclaiming herself the "Publick Universal Friend." Though she could not read, she proved herself divinely inspired by her knowledge of the Bible, all of which she could quote from memory, and her speech was so laden with God's truth, so her followers said, that she won the devotion of hundreds. Because she was darkly beautiful and emotionally persuasive, more than two hundred of these migrated with her to the country of the Finger Lakes shortly after 1790. There, in her purple robe and white beaver hat—low-crowned and broad-brimmed—she ruled her people as a queen who derived her authority from the Almighty.

Her palace was a large white house on the shores of Crooked Lake (now Keuka), and there seven pretty handmaidens sought to fulfill her every wish. At her right sat lovely and youthful Rachel Malin—heir apparent to her kingdom—and at her left, in the white robes of a prophet, James Parker, "the spirit of Elijah," who was accustomed on occasions he thought propitious to draw his girdle so tight that his belly swelled out above it like a balloon, then to announce that he was filled with the wind of prophecy and deliver oracular utterances with an assurance frequently accepted by "The Friend" and her people as proceeding from direct communication with the Lord.

In 1816 Jemima Wilkinson was fifty-eight, and her striking beauty had vanished. She would die for the second time ("leave time," she called it) in three years, but she was still the autocratic leader of her people. Young Joe Smith heard much of her upon his arrival

in the drumlin country and, since she was still very active in attending to what she considered the needs of her flock, he may have seen her, pitifully fat and dropsical, behind the fluttering damask curtains of her couch, which shone like an uptilted half-moon above wheels that glittered through the dust of the turnpike.

It is unlikely that the spindling, yellow-haired lad, tall for his years, dreamed in those days of ever becoming the third of the region's religious "originals" whose lack of formal education rendered their achievements in the eyes of those who believed in them inexplicable save through the miraculous power of God. Nevertheless, a few years later when he was bitterly assailed as an ignorant though cunning charlatan, he may have taken some comfort from the fact that hundreds of good and honest people had believed in the divine origin of the words that came from the mouths of Rachel Baker and the Publick Universal Friend.

For the two years that followed their exodus from Vermont the Smith family earned and saved in and around lively Palmyra. There were wells to be dug, farms to be cleared, harvests to be reaped, and father Joseph and his sons were employable. When such work was scarce they diversified the articles for sale at their shop by making split-wood baskets, kegs, churns, wooden flails for threshing. By 1818 they had enough money to make a down payment on one hundred acres of wild land two miles south of Palmyra and near the largest of the drumlins. Here, they raised a substantial log house, and when a thaw signaled the approach of spring, they tapped so many of their sugar maples, it is recorded, that they manufactured from one season's flow of sap three and a half tons of maple sugar, which made them winners of a bounty of fifty dollars as the leading producers in Wayne County.

Joseph was now tall enough and strong enough to do a man's job. How he happened to be in the woods that edged the Susquehanna River at Great Bend, Pennsylvania, is not known, but the writings of a companion who lived in that area at the time, one J. B. Buck, recall an important event that colored the rest of his life. "Joe Smith was here lumbering soon after my marriage which was in 1818, some years before he took to 'peeping' and before diggings were commenced under his direction. These were ideas he gained later."

Mr. Buck said that Jack Belcher (the Belchers came from Union Hill in Gibson Township) had shown Joseph a stone which he said would give to those who looked upon it in darkness clairvoyant powers. Jack had bought this "seeing stone," as he called it, when he was working with the saltmakers at Salina in York State. Mr. Buck wrote that he had often seen the Belcher stone himself. "It was a green stone with brown, irregular spots on it. It was a little longer than a goose's egg, and about the same thickness."

Such a talisman was not a new concept among Pennsylvania and New York settlers at this time. James Fenimore Cooper in his novel *The Pioneers,* which depicted Cooperstown as it was in 1793, wrote that one of his characters (Jotham) "acknowledged before he died that his reasons for believing in a mine were extracted from the lips of a sybil who, by looking in a magic glass, was enabled to discover the hidden treasures of the earth." The author then added the explanatory note, "Such superstition was frequent in the new settlements." These sentences were written during 1823, a year when Joseph was especially active in "glass looking" (the popular phrase for the use of seeing-stones), and would seem to indicate that when Joseph beheld Belcher's purchase, such aids to psychic vision had been in popular use in America for at least a generation. There is the possibility at least that reports of Joseph's "money-digging" on the Susquehanna just south of the New York border at the very time Cooper was writing his book at the river's source had brought clairvoyance to the writer's attention.

Belcher let it be known that his green and brown treasure was for sale. He added, as proof of its value, that when he had brought it back to his Pennsylvania home and covered it with his hat, his little boy, who had been first to peep into the darkness under the brim, had seen it glowing like a lighted candle. Upon looking a second time, said the father, his son exclaimed, "I've found my hatchet," and ran to the spot where that article had been lying lost for two years. After that the boy had been asked by many neighbors to look into the stone and tell them where to find things they had misplaced, and he had "succeeded marvellously," even in tracing the wanderings of a lost child, who, when found, was dead from starvation.

That this prize would excite in a boy of Joseph's temperament a desire for possessing it was inevitable. He bought the stone, wrote Mr. Buck, though he did not say how much of the young lumberman's hardearned and scanty wages was exchanged for it. Joseph at once tested it and reported that he saw treasures in the earth near Red Rock—where the likeness of a giant chief, painted by a prehistoric Indian artist, decorated a perpendicular stone surface beside the Susquehanna.

Disappointment in the project was attributed not to the inefficacy of the stone but to the diggers' failure to maintain strict silence while at work—one of the primary rules of the then-current, orally transmitted manual of treasure-digging. Mr. Buck said Joseph claimed that because of this error "the enchantment removed the deposits."

If Mr. Buck's reminiscences are trustworthy, and they have the ring of truth, Joseph seems to have bought his first seeing-stone only a short time before he beheld, according to his own testimony, the vision which first revealed his appointment to his divine mission. He had hardly returned from the Susquehanna's wooded banks when a wild religious revival, a sort of spiritual forest fire, swept into Palmyra from the eastern coastal states, where it had been raging for months. Ardent, ambitious Jesse Townsend, a recent graduate of Yale, began it with the intensity and fervor of youth; and success brought to his side a fellow Presbyterian, Preacher Stockton from East Palmyra. At once, and at the invitation of these evangelists, the Baptist minister joined in and so did Methodist Preacher McLane. Soon, however, what had seemed an inspired alliance of the three denominations in the cause of Protestant Christianity, turned into strife.

Fourteen-year-old Joseph found himself in an agonizing quandary. His mother Lucy, his brothers Hyrum and Samuel Harrison, and his sister Sophronia were all, as he wrote later in 1838, "proselyted to the Presbyterian faith." Nevertheless, he had been so moved by the strenuous appeals of the Methodist spellbinders that, as one of his boyhood schoolmates remarked years later, "after catching a spark of Methodism in the camp-meeting, away down in the woods, on the Vienna road, he was a very passable exhorter in evening meetings."

The bitter animosity which each of the sects directed toward the others gave the boy no peace.

"In the midst of this war of words and tumult of opinions, I often said to myself, 'What is to be done?' " A chance reading of the Epistle of James, 1:5, gave him the answer: "If any of you lack wisdom, let him

A strong revivalist spirit swept through his York State area when Joseph Smith was a boy, but a vision from heaven told him, he later claimed, to join none of the sects, for "all their creeds were an abomination."

ask of God, that giveth to all men liberally, and upbraideth not; and it shall be given him."

Joseph said it was on a clear and sunny morning of early May in the year 1820 when he decided to take this advice. The lanky, tow-haired youngster had found a secret, quiet place, and like many another boy of his age he took pride in feeling that by right of discovery it was his own. A quarter of a mile behind his home he climbed a gentle slope edged with young beeches and a tangle of shrubbery, to a summit where stood a company of tall sugar maples. An opening among the leaf-hung branches allowed a shaft of yellow sunlight to penetrate the shade. There was a stillness here, overwrought with almost inaudible sounds—bird calls, the hum of bees, the whisper of foliage as the air drifted in a movement too gentle to be called a breeze. Here was a refuge from the pressures exerted by the shouting preachers, the emotional hymns, the outcries of hysterical penitents. Here, as he lay on his back in the shade of the high maples, he believed peace might enter his tortured mind. Not peace, he reported later, but darkness enveloped him: "It seemed to me for a time as if I were doomed to sudden destruction . . . and at the very moment when I was ready to sink into despair . . . just at this moment of great alarm, I saw a pillar of light exactly over my head."

Consciousness of the material world left him, he said, without his being aware of its going; for all seemed real as before except for movement among the tiny particles that danced within the gleaming column, a massive changing into distinguishable forms of light existing within light. He saw, or dreamed he saw, two figures suspended there; heard, or dreamed he heard, their voices.

"I asked the personages, who stood above me in the light, which of all the sects was right . . . I was answered . . . all their creeds were an abomination."

When the luminous gods had uttered their message and vanished from the bright shaft, Joseph said, he came to himself again, lying on his back and looking up to heaven. His mind had been freed of torment.

The vision and the voices, despite their intimations that he was chosen to fulfill a divine purpose, had not, however, created a sense of consecration to a mission promised but unexplained. After he had told one of the Methodist evangelists of his experience and been ridiculed for his pains, he put aside the idea of conversion to any denomination. Being a sociable, growing adolescent, he gave himself over to such enjoyments as came naturally to a youth of his time and in his region. Even the first visit of the tall angel, Moroni, when he was seventeen, did not deter him from worldly pleasures. In his late twenties, after the birth of Mormonism, Joseph frankly admitted this fact: "As is common to most, or all youths, I fell into many vices and follies . . . and those imperfections to which I allude, and for which I have often had occasion to lament, were a light and, too often, vain mind exhibiting a foolish and trifling conversation."

Most available descriptions of Joseph Smith as a boy were written after he had become the founder of the Mormon Church. They show resentment that such a youth became important enough to command public attention, shock at his claims, which were regarded as sacrilegious, suspicion that he was a charlatan and to be regarded with amused contempt. Any testimony in his favor could be regarded, then, as unwilling and therefore worth considering. A learned historian, O. Turner, who recalled Joseph's walking in to Palmyra village from the Smith farm two miles out on Stafford Street, remembered that the boy once a week strolled into the office of the old Palmyra *Register* for his father's paper and sometimes did odd jobs at Scovell's store. "I can see him now in my mind's eye," reported Daniel Hendrix, who had been a typesetter in those days, "with his torn and patched trousers held to his form by a pair of suspenders made out of sheeting, with his calico shirt as dirty and black as the earth, and his uncombed hair sticking through the holes in his old battered hat."

This lake-country prototype of Huckleberry Finn combined in his person strangely fascinating qualities. Said Hendrix, "Joe had a jovial easy don't-care way about him that made him a lot of warm friends." Pomeroy Tucker, one of the owners of the Palmyra *Sentinel,* remembered that the boy was proverbially good-natured, yet he was never known to laugh. All witnesses agreed that he was both imaginative and articulate. And there was his ability as an exhorter, to which Turner referred. To quote Hendrix again:

He was a good talker and would have made a fine stump-speaker if he had had the training. He was known among the young men I was associated with as a romancer of the first water. I never knew so ignorant a man as Joe to have such a fertile imagination. He could never tell a common occurrence in his daily life without embellishing the story with his imagination; yet I remember he was grieved one day when old Parson Reed told Joe he was going to hell for his lying habits.

From these descriptions emerges a personality not at all inconsistent with the New England whence Joseph Smith came nor the area in which he grew to manhood. The narrator who told exaggerated tales with a straight face was a widely admired figure of the time. The title "biggest liar in the county" was highly prized and eagerly sought by every narrator of popular oral fiction. Joseph's grandfather, Solomon Mack, was just such a storyteller. The superstitions of his neighbors had given Joseph's impressionable and eager mind fascinating materials, and from them he had fashioned a world of miracle and wonder. Hence, he could well be grieved when Parson Reed confused his creative literary imaginings with immoral lying. A psychiatrist today might add a note to modern concepts of the boy upon reading a contemporary's testimony that "At times he was melancholy and sedate, as often hilarious and mirthful," though the sentence can hardly be accepted as justifying any conclusion.

Since the great majority of his community identified all semblances of the supernatural as the works of either the devil or the Lord, it was inevitable that he should do the same. A contemporary said that Joseph told him his power to use his peep-stone as an instrument of clairvoyance came from God. If he believed this, his occult practices after his first vision, which were harshly criticized, would seem consistent. Since he was more sensitive, fanciful, and articulate than those who inhabited the small suspicion-ridden world in which he lived, it is not surprising that he won spreading fame for supernatural gifts. Among those who later turned against him with bitter words were men whose greed for buried gold had led them to believe that he possessed occult powers and to employ his services as a clairvoyant.

Whatever his motivations, Joseph was still susceptible to the wonder of small stones. In 1822, he and others were digging a well for the Chase family in nearby Manchester, when, at a depth of more than twenty feet, appeared an opaque stone "of a whitish glassy appearance" and shaped "like a child's foot."

This gleaming grotesque so captured his speculative mind that he bought it at once and enlisted its magic. When it was in his hat and his face was down over it to exclude all light from outside, said neighbor Joseph Capron, he could see by its radiance objects of great wonder— "ghosts, infernal spirits, mountains of gold and silver."

Apparently the discovery and purchase of the "child's foot" stone added to Joseph's reputation. Though only seventeen, he possessed the recognized implements of a glass-looker, and his was the name that came immediately to mind through-

out the region whenever there was talk of buried treasure and the spells exerted over it by concealers long dead. According to later testimony of his neighbors, he had acquired much of his comprehensive knowledge of occult lore from a peripatetic magician, conjurer, and fortune teller named Walters, who had no sooner wandered into the nearby town of Sodus than he had been jailed for the crime of "juggling." Undiscouraged by the coldness of his welcome, Walters let it be known that for three dollars a day he would make use of his supernatural gifts, his divining rods ("peach, witch-hazel, and mineral"), his crystal spheres, and his stuffed toads, in finding Indian gold and chests of Spanish coins lying beneath the surface of many an otherwise unproductive farm. A disapproving local journal, the Palmyra *Reflector,* reported that Walters once "assembled his nightly band of money-diggers in the town of Manchester, at a point designated in his magical book, and drawing a circle around laborers with the point of an old sword and using sundry other incantations" sacrificed a rooster to propitiate the spirit of the place, but all his ritual proved to no avail.

When Walters had resumed his vagabondage, the *Reflector* ironically and jocosely suggested that the mantle of the town's former mystic had fallen upon young Joseph Smith. When in 1833 Joseph, founder of the Church of Jesus Christ of Latter-day Saints, excommunicated from that body in Kirtland, Ohio, handsome Philaster Hurlbut for "unchristian conduct" toward the females of the sect, Philaster raced to Palmyra to beg from more than a hundred of the prophet's former neighbors affidavits exposing Joseph's sinful conduct in the years before he claimed the discovery of the golden plates.

While the statements obtained are highly suspect (since most of them do not repeat information given by others, and since all are couched in Hurlbut's style) they furnish an authoritative manual of the wildly poetic folk-concepts with which Joseph's brain boiled during his adolescence. Many who testified against

On September 21, 1823, Joseph Smith later asserted, he first saw the angel Moroni, who directed him to a cache of mysterious golden plates on a hillside on the Smith farm.

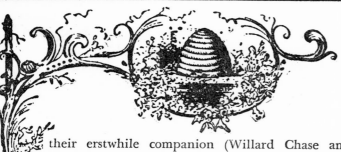

their erstwhile companion (Willard Chase among them) had firmly believed in the superstitions they now jealously cited as proofs of the wickedness and deceit of the boy whose mind had absorbed them. According to the affidavits, Joseph had at various times offered the following suggestions to treasure diggers:

The best time for digging money is the summer when the sun's heat draws ancient coffers "near the top of the ground."

A chest of gold watches lay in the earth of Joe Capron's farm, but it was retrievable only if a man brandishing a burnished sword marched the surface above it to protect the diggers from assaults by the devil himself.

In a hill on the Cuyler farm was a cave "containing an immense value of gold and silver, stand of arms, also a saddle for a camel hanging on a peg at one side of the cave" ("the ancient inhabitants of this country used camels instead of horses"). There were other caves, too, and one sheltered "barrels and hogsheads of coined silver and gold—bars of gold, golden images, brass kettles filled with gold and silver—gold candlesticks, swords," all in charge of spirits clad in ancient dress.

To find such riches, hire a glass-looker, blindfold him, and bid him kneel. Then hold before him at eye-level a tall white hat in which his seer-stone lies concealed and he will see the place you seek.

To possess the treasure take a black sheep to the spot, cut its throat, and lead it bleeding in a circle that the red drippings may penetrate the earth and appease the ghastly guards below.

Or, dressed in black and riding a black horse with a switch tail, gallop to the place and demand the treasure in a certain name. As the chest rises from the earth, lift the lid and take your prize, but beware the blinking toad beside it that in a trice becomes a man and knocks you three or four rods with one blow.

New impulses swept western New York as the year 1825 began. Not since the coming of the Yankees exiled by 1816's cold summer had the countryside been so stirred. Already commercial craft were plying long sections of Governor De Witt Clinton's man-made river, which was to be completed and opened in the fall, and profits were said to exceed the golden dreams of their owners. The Erie Canal towns near the Smith family home were boiling with expectations.

From the east to nearby Sodus on the shore of Lake Ontario came a colony of Shakers, and immediately the nervous religious ferment of the past decade intensified. The Shakers' insistence on asceticism, celibacy, cleanliness, and quiet contrasted strangely with their worshipful rituals. Visitors reported their religious exercises included dancing and whirling and marching, which moved them to such ecstasies that participants broke from the pattern and, receiving "the gift of tongues," howled out long passages of unintelligible gibberish.

From the east, too, came the Irish laborers on the canal, and their presence in the miasmic Montezuma swamps had added the melancholy of their native music and the humor of their tall tales to local folklore. The ghostly voices of malaria-slain diggers called at night above the bogs between Geneva and Seneca Falls, and the bills of mosquitoes, blown up by Celtic fancy to the size of well drills, pierced the iron sides of sap kettles.

Spring was slipping into summer when out of the west on the placid waters of the new channel floated a gala craft, bearing the old Marquis de Lafayette. The boy-hero of the American Revolution, now sixty-eight, had returned in the previous year to the land he had fought for, and his triumphal tour of it was soon to end. He had given the lake-country towns short notice of his visit, but they were ready for him. At Rochester a flotilla of twelve flower-strewn, pennant-hung barges awaited his arrival. Brass bands on their decks crashed into "Hail, Columbia" and "Hail to the Chief," and an artillery company let go air-shattering salutes as his boat slipped under bridges laden with cheering, waving admirers. The canal's banks were thronged, the city's roof tops covered, its windows packed, as the populace raised "shouts of joyful acclamation."

The cannoneers of Canandaigua, gathered hastily at their guns, welcomed the tall wizened general that evening with salvos heard far across Canandaigua Lake, and the town's spacious hotel produced a feast for one hundred distinguished guests. By ten o'clock next morning a lake-to-lake journey had been made, and the nation's most welcome visitor, in an elegant barouche drawn by six milk-white horses, rolled into Geneva, heralded by massed bands and the "roar of ordinance" echoing over Seneca's waters. When Lafayette re-embarked on the canal that evening at Syracuse, having covered seventy-five miles by coach in twenty-four hours, the towns through which he had passed were already contentedly regarding the day's efforts as only a rehearsal of the autumn celebration soon to come when the waters of Lake Erie would at last be linked with those of the broad Atlantic and the harvests of the boundless West might be dispatched on waterways to the far-scattered markets of the world.

On October 26 the *Seneca Chief*, new canal packet, made her way from Lake Erie into the completed "Hellespont of the West," hailed by thousands of the citizens of Buffalo. The *Young Lion of the West*, bearing in cages on her decks two wolves, a fawn, a fox, four raccoons, and two eagles, awaited her in Rochester. As the water parade made majestic progress through the drumlin country, farmers and townsfolk raced across the fertile fields, described only a few years before as "so barren 'twould make an owl weep to fly over them," to become witnesses of a new wonder of the world. Workers who had labored during the day were guided to the procession by fireworks bursting in the night sky. Golden reflections emanated from the water, for an unending aisle of barrels, like dark stubby candles, spurted flames above the channel, and the air was thick with the pungent, almost choking, smell of burning tar. Distant gunfire produced a steady thudding, which was interrupted now and then by the reverberating crash of a nearby cannon. Figures appeared on the boat decks waving toward the shores, and excited spectators tried to identify the governor of the state of New York, De Witt Clinton; the distinguished, long-haired scientist, Samuel Latham Mitchell; the mayors, judges, professors of neighboring towns.

While there is no specific proof that nineteen-year-old Joseph Smith, money digger and farmhand, saw either of 1825's wildly applauded spectacles, there can be no doubt that they had an influence on him, as they did on everyone else in western New York. Since he was the grandson of two veterans of the Revolution, and Canandaigua was a scant nine miles from his home, there is a strong possibility that he made the opportunity to see the noble Frenchman and his cortege somewhere along the route. And being of the nature he was, it is unlikely that Joseph missed the ceremonies attendant upon the consummation of the "marriage of the waters" which had been awaited by all the area for eight long years. Perhaps, indeed, his love of parades and uniforms and pageantry, patent in the days when he himself received the huzzas of a worshipful populace, stemmed from those moments of that magic, long summer when the visions of the shining barouche and the prancing white steeds, the light-filled canal and the elegant packets, flashed upon his eyes; when his ears were enchanted by the brassy chorusing of the bands and the thunderous booming of the guns.

In mid-autumn of 1825, Farmer Josiah Stowel of South Bainbridge, a Chenango County town on the Susquehanna, just north of the Pennsylvania border, traveled over the long western New York State hills to Palmyra. He had two purposes in mind—to visit his relatives and to talk with the glass-looker, Joseph Smith, who, he had heard, might be able to divine the place on his acres where Spaniards had long ago mined silver. He offered Joseph fourteen dollars a month "and found" to go to his farm with him, and, in a few days the boy, his father, and Stowel were on their way. At the end of their journey the Smiths were "put to board" at the home of a prosperous hunter, Isaac Hale, who lived across the state line in the Pennsylvania town named Harmony.

The Hale household was a big one the fall that Joseph Smith was a part of it. The father, a Vermonter then in his sixty-fourth year, had sired five sons and three daughters. Thirty-eight years of hunting on the New York State frontier had developed him into a familiar American type—the experienced and wise old woodsman—much the same character as the fictional "Leatherstocking" whom the novelist James Fenimore Cooper (living not far away, also close to the Susquehanna) was creating. Isaac Hale and his boys must have used all their stealth and woodcraft and hunted early and late in Ichabod Swamp, on Turkey Hill, and along the Starucca and Pig-pen creeks to fetch enough meat for the family and treasure hunters. Nine years afterward Isaac recorded that the Smiths (father and son) "and several other money-diggers boarded at my house . . . digging for a mine that they supposed had been opened and worked by the Spaniards many years since." At first the hunter had believed in the project, but he later said that Joseph had disillusioned and disgusted him by announcing that his peep-stone was failing him because of a more powerful counter-enchantment.

Among the women serving the hungry men in those weeks of night digging, a slim, tall, dark daughter of the house had caught Joseph's eye. By nature twenty-two-year-old Emma Hale was taciturn and reserved, and she was soon sitting, wide-eyed and silent, beside

In a setting which Smith later described in terms reminiscent of the Last Supper, he organized the Mormon Church April 6, 1830, in the Fayette, N. Y., home of Peter Whitmer, Sr.

Joseph while he unburdened his mind of the wonders that teemed within it.

When the expedition, despairing, shouldered spades and departed in mid-November, its glass-looker went back to Josiah Stowel's farm, but he returned again and again throughout the snowy winter to woo the hunter's daughter. Meanwhile, he worked for Stowel, went to school, and kept on peering into his dark talisman to behold in its glow, if he could, the riches his employer confidently expected him to find. Whenever the weather allowed, Josiah sent word to his diggers to assemble, and after darkness had fallen Joseph led them across the river flats to scramble up the steeps of the surrounding hills. Countless old coins, the diggers dreamed, lay buried on Bond Mountain, heavy gold on Monument Hill, and under a slope near the Bainbridge farm salt-laden waters burbled.

Torches flared on the ridges above the valley towns while the diggers recited incantations to break the spells laid upon the ground into which they sank their spades. Then, as spring began, one, Peter Bridgeman, intolerant of such goings-on, swore out a warrant for the arrest of Joseph Smith as "a disorderly person and an impostor."

Joseph was brought before a justice of the peace at Bainbridge on March 20, 1826. Of the five witnesses at his trial, three told of their certainty that the defendant could "divine things" by "looking into a hat at his dark-colored stone." One of these said that Joseph had told him how a money trunk was situated, and that after he had dug down several feet for it he struck upon something sounding like a board or plank. At this moment, the witness testified, Joseph remembered that the last time he looked into his stone he had seen the two Indians who had buried the trunk quarreling until one slew the other and threw his body into the hole beside the trunk where it remained as a spirit-guard. It had proved its protective power, the witness continued, for as the digging went on the trunk kept sinking and remained constantly at about the same distance from the diggers.

Despite the testimony of the three who believed in Joseph's mystic powers, however, two scoffers appearing for the prosecution found more favor with the judge. The trial record states, "The Court finds the defendant guilty."

No report of the sentence has been found. If there was one, it must have been either light or suspended,

for Joseph continued his work on the Stowel farm throughout the rest of the year. Isaac Hale, on being asked by Joseph for consent to his marrying Emma, replied with a stormy No. No stranger, he said, and certainly not a glass-looker, could marry a daughter of his. And so throughout the summer of 1826 Joseph, whenever he could leave the Stowel farm, made journeys southward that ended in clandestine lovers' meetings.

It was in the Indian summer days of Joseph's courtship of Emma Hale that there befell a third event which would have an even greater aftereffect on him than the pomp and show of the two pageants that had stirred the countryside. Whether the young lover was at his father's home during the second week of September, 1826, or surreptitiously meeting his sweetheart by Susquehanna's winding stream is not known, nor is it very important, for the story of what happened in western New York during those few days was to shock the whole nation and influence the thoughts not only of Joseph Smith but of thousands of other Americans for years to come.

William Morgan, a hotheaded Virginian who had served as captain under General Andrew Jackson at the Battle of New Orleans, had settled with his wife and children at Batavia, official seat of Genesee County. Morgan claimed to be a high ranking member of the Ancient Order of Masons and persuaded neighboring fellow members to apply to a chapter of Royal Arch Masons in nearby Le Roy for permission to establish a similar lodge in Batavia. Somehow, perhaps because he was a hard-drinking, boastful man, the applicants suspected that Morgan was not as high in the fraternity as he claimed, and would not allow him to sign their petition. The insult enraged him and, under his Virginian's code, cried for revenge. A friend of his, Colonel David Miller, was also a veteran of the recent war and a dissident Mason. Miller was owner of the town newspaper, and the two ex-soldiers made no secret of the fact that they planned to print an exposé of the secret rites and purposes of Masonry.

In the middle of the night of Friday, September 8, forty masked men in fantastic dress marched in quick, catlike steps in the dust of a Batavia street and halted before Miller's print shop. At once flame leapt within it, and the vandals took up again their muffled tread. A tramp who had chosen to sleep in an empty stagecoach broke the silence then with loud cries. Lamps flickered on in the windows of Batavia, and doors slammed as men raced from their homes. Their attack on the blaze succeeded. The presses were saved and could still print Morgan's book.

The Masons who had decided to take into their own hands the carrying out of such horrific penalties for violation of their fraternal pledges met secretly to plan other ways of thwarting their enemy. On Sunday morning a Canandaigua magistrate issued a warrant for Morgan's arrest on charges of stealing a shirt. A constable and a posse of five reached Batavia that night. In the morning they arrested Morgan, beating down Colonel Miller's frantic efforts to protect him, and began their return journey with their prisoner. The next day Morgan pleaded that he had only borrowed the shirt and was released, but his prosecutors quickly charged him with failure to pay a tavern bill of $2.69 when last in Canandaigua and he was remanded to jail.

On the heavy, hot night of Tuesday, September 12, repeated knocking brought the jailer's wife to her door, where suave men told her they had come to pay Morgan's debt and procure his release. The woman said her husband was absent, and that releases late at night were not customary, but the men finally persuaded her to let the prisoner go. As Morgan walked down the jail steps, there was a sudden scuffle, then a man's voice crying "Help! Murder!" to the quiet, moonlit town. A yellow, curtained carriage drawn by a team of fast-trotting grays flashed into the empty street and drew up to the jailer's curb. For a moment men struggled in its black shadow. Then there were no more cries—only the sound of horses' hoofs beating the powderlike, crumbling earth of the road's surface.

By morning the yellow wheels had rolled as far as Hanford's Tavern, just outside of Rochester. There waited a team of bays hitched to another carriage, black and funereal.

The journey reached its end at the small, round powder-chamber of old Fort Niagara, where the captors locked up their charge. Few doubt now that soon thereafter they murdered him and threw his body into the Niagara River.

To a lovesick young man these events, at the time of their happening, may have meant little. Nevertheless, the crime and the shocked talk that it aroused were to make a lasting impression on Joseph Smith.

By the end of the year the lovers could wait no longer. They sought the aid of Josiah Stowel, and it was eagerly given. On January 18 of the new year of 1827, Joseph met Emma secretly for the last time and drove her to South Bainbridge. There, in the home of Squire Tarbill, they were married by Tarbill himself. Almost immediately, and probably to escape the wrath of the bride's father, they set out for Manchester, where they received a hearty and approving welcome. The neighbors were too excited at this time by the Canandaigua murder trial of the men who had attacked and transported William Morgan, to give much attention to a runaway bride, and Joseph, now facing responsibility as a husband and potential father, happily set about the farm duties allotted to him by his father and his brothers. These, to a young man whose life had already proved his intolerance of boredom, must have seemed dull indeed, but he was buoyed up by a consciousness that before long something would happen—an event so momentous that it would change the course of his life in miraculous ways. Whether, as nearly two million good Mormons believe today, he was waiting in awe and reverence for the return of the angel who had promised him that in September he would at last receive the book of golden pages lying in the nearby hill, or whether, as skeptics have suspected, he was planning the perpetration of the most amazing hoax in history, the spring and summer of 1827 must have been a time of almost breathless anticipation for the tall and thoughtful bridegroom as he went about his homely and over-familiar tasks. Seedtime came and went; the heat of summer danced above the hills and waters; the September harvest was at hand.

At last came the moonless night of the twenty-first. Outside their home in the nearby Cayuga County town of Aurelius, a twenty-six-year-old carpenter, painter, and joiner, Brigham Young, and his young wife, Miriam, stared long at the western sky. Years afterward this man, whose name would be linked throughout posterity with that of Joseph Smith, remembered that they had seen a strange light there which was "perfectly clear and remained for several hours." As they continued to look, "it formed into men as if there were great armies in the West; and I then saw in the North West armies of men come up. They would march to the South West and then go out of sight. It was a very remarkable occurrence. It passed on, and continued perhaps about two hours." At about that moment Joseph Smith had prepared himself to make what he later said was his fourth annual ascent of the Hill of Cumorah.

Among the first to whom Joseph Smith preached were American Indians. They were descended, the Book of Mormon said, from Palestinian stock whose nobler branch produced the prophet Mormon and his son Moroni.

The Electoral College

CONTINUED FROM PAGE 18

thereof may direct." They would meet in their respective states, on a day fixed by Congress, and vote for two men (at least one being from another state) but make no distinction between them. If any candidate received a majority of the votes of the whole number of Electors, he would become President. The runner-up would be Vice President—an office newly devised.

Significantly, it was considered that not once in twenty times (one man thought not once in fifty) would the Electors give a majority to one man. After all, the country was large—there were thirteen states, some of them weeks of travel apart—and how would a man in, say, Georgia know the name, let alone the qualifications, of a candidate from Massachusetts? If no candidate received a majority, or if two or more were tied for first place, then the choice of President would fall to the House of Representatives; if there was a tie for second, the Senate would choose the Vice President. It was probably this proviso that reconciled the parliamentary supremacists to the scheme.

The conviction sustaining them all was that in any event the Electors would be the cream of the social, economic, and intellectual elite of each state, hence best qualified to exercise superior judgment, whether as Electors—if they could agree on one man, as they were sure to do in the case of George Washington—or as nominators, in which case they would be able to give the House a number of good men to choose from.

Alexander Hamilton was so captivated by this ingenious contrivance that he wrote (in the sixty-eighth *Federalist,* devoted to it) that "I hesitate not to affirm that if the manner of it be not perfect, it is at least excellent. . . . Nothing was more to be desired than that every practicable obstacle should be opposed to cabal, intrigue, and corruption."

In the first election (1789), in which Washington was by common consent unanimously chosen to be Chief Magistrate, the Federalist leaders agreed that John Adams should be the choice of the Electors for Vice President. Adams had many virtues to qualify him for the post, but his chief asset was that he came from Massachusetts, which state was second only to Virginia in the number of electoral votes it commanded—and George Washington was from Virginia. (How many smoke-filled rooms have since then heard the balancing-off of candidates' states of origin, to the disregard of their "other talents," and the "different kind of merit" Hamilton had said a candidate would have to have to qualify for the high office of President?)

But Adams and Washington had suffered from some differences during the war, and so the latter had first to be sounded out on whether he found the former acceptable. And though Washington continued right through his Farewell Address to reprobate the "spirit of party," he did not rebuke his friends over this show of it. Instead, he cautiously replied that "having taken it for granted that the person elected for that important post would be a true Federalist," he was "altogether disposed to acquiesce in the prevailing sentiments of the Electors without any unbecoming preference, or incurring any unnecessary ill-will." Washington had presided at the Constitutional Convention; he knew as well as anyone what the intent had been with respect to the freedom of Electors to make uninstructed choices.

As for Hamilton, he enjoyed a mutual antipathy with Adams, and he honored his warm regard for the obstacles placed in the way of cabal and intrigue by sending special messengers to New Jersey, Connecticut, and Pennsylvania to get Electors to withhold votes from Adams, on the pretext that Adams might obtain more votes than Washington, and thus become President.

Sic transeunt high ideals.

Not to be outdone by the Federalists, the Antifederalist leaders—notably Thomas Jefferson, Aaron Burr, and George Clinton—applied themselves diligently to unifying a collection of local factions and personal cliques into a national party. They determined early that whatever else a party may have in the way of program and personalities, it needs machinery. They constructed it. They also in due time abandoned the negative name, to become the "Democratic-Republican" (later shortened to Republican and in Jackson's time changed to Democratic) party. By 1800 the machine—a tight ensemble of state organizations—was ready for road-testing. (Tammany Hall swung the balance that year, and remains a still-standing monument to Burr's industry.) This apparatus delivered to the Jefferson-Burr ticket a solid package of seventy-three faithful, instructed Electors—a clear, safe majority.

One small—oversight? Whether on Burr's part it was intentional or inadvertent will never be known; Jefferson thought the danger had been carefully forestalled. However it was, all seventy-three faithful Electors, directed by the Constitution to vote for two men, voted for *both* Jefferson and Burr.

So there was a tie. Whatever the later politicians desired, the framers of the Constitution had been clear in their intentions—that any man an Elector voted for should have an equal chance with any other candidate to be President. They did not even specify separate qualifications for vice presidential candidates. The Vice President (though many opposed having such an office at all) was to be simply the near-miss President. And if the Electors on their first try could not give the edge to one man, then they must leave it to the House.

And there the Jefferson-Burr tie went, to be received with diabolical glee. The majority was Democratic-Republican by six members, but the composition of the sixteen state delegations was such that the Jeffersonians dominated only an exact half of them; the Federalists controlled six, and two were evenly divided. Most of the Federalist congressmen had been defeated in the last elections and were limping out the remaining weeks of their expiring terms. Here was a Heaven-sent opportunity for them to heap disaster on their Antifederalist foes. They would try to make Burr President! This, they were sure, would destroy the Democratic-Republican party.

Hamilton was equally sure that it would destroy the nation as well. As soon as he realized their intentions, he went energetically to work among his fellow Federalists to avert the catastrophe. He hated but respected Jefferson; he hated and despised Burr.

At first his efforts seemed futile. The Federalist-controlled states went to Burr, preventing Jefferson's election by one state. This deadlock prevailed for nearly a week, through thirty-five ballots. Finally it broke. No Federalist gave his vote to Jefferson, but enough of them refrained from voting at all to enable their Democratic-Republican colleagues to add two states to Jefferson's total, and give him the Presidency. Burr became Vice President, and never thereafter anything else. For him, the incident spelled political doom. For Hamilton, the vehemence of his intervention against Burr led inexorably to his death at Burr's hands three years later. For the Federalists, the blow from the new political party (fumble notwithstanding) was mortal.

An immediate consequence was the Twelfth Amendment, remedying two of the Constitution's flaws that had been exposed. Electors were now required to give *separate* votes for President and Vice President. And of necessity, it now added the injunction that candidates for the latter office must have the same qualifications as those for the former.

These oversights were rectified sixteen years after the adoption of the Constitution; 129 more years were to elapse before the Twentieth Amendment would deprive congressional lame ducks of the capacity to do mischief whose consequences they would not have to bear. That later amendment would also shorten, but insufficiently, the perilous lapse of time between election and inauguration of a new administration.

Other defects remain, and efforts to correct them continue. The most determined reforms concern themselves with the electoral process itself. Some, however, attack the nominating system as well—now a hodgepodge of state-prescribed contrivances for choosing delegates to national party conventions.

The forerunner of this less-than-ideal system was even more objectionable; it was called King Caucus. This monster was born in that same election campaign of 1800, and its father was Alexander Hamilton. With his foes in the ascendancy, he was desperate for a means of curing the dissension—aggravated by the recent death of Washington—that was destroying his own party from within. He therefore urged the Federalist congressional leaders to move in and take control of the presidential election.

Congressional party caucus on legislative matters had already become habitual. By usage, majority decision had become binding on all. Now, at Hamilton's insistence, this irregular but institutionalized device was to embrace the election of the Executive as well. The Federalist congressmen met in secret and nominated John Adams and Charles C. Pinckney. Their power not only to choose the candidates but to control the Electors is evidenced by the canvass: the Federalist Electors gave all their 65 votes to Adams. *They* did not blunder; Pinckney received only 64, although Hamilton, because of his old dislike for Adams, had urged their equal support.

Word of the secret meeting leaked out. The Democratic-Republican press noisily protested the "arrogance of a number of Congress to assemble as an electioneering caucus to control the citizens in their constitutional rights." This pious condemnation did not, however, inhibit the Antifederalists in Congress. They also met in secret, to nominate Jefferson and Burr. By the following election, 1804, they were emboldened to dispense with stealth, and conducted their meeting with all the punctilio of a parliament.

Alas for high hopes! In the sixty-eighth *Federalist,* Hamilton had stressed that "the Executive should be independent for his continuance in the office on all but the people themselves. He might otherwise be tempted to sacrifice his duty to his complaisance for those whose favor was necessary to the duration of his official consequence." (Gouverneur Morris had expressed the same concern in other words.) The bitter prophecy came true for—of all people—James Madison, Hamilton's chief coauthor of the *Federalist* papers, and archadvocate of separation of powers.

The pressures that had been building toward the War of 1812 came to bear on President Madison as his first term drew to a close. He had no stomach for armed conflict, and he felt a peaceful solution could be negotiated. Had he persisted, the war might have been averted, since the British lifted the blockade for American ships on June 16, 1812. But the news did not reach Congress before the eighteenth, when, in response to Madison's reluctant message, it voted a declaration of war.

It was a message extorted from Madison by the caucus. James Fisk, a Democratic-Republican congressman from Vermont, reportedly called on the President to say that the country felt provoked to war. If he resisted the "popular will," the Federalists threatened to win the forthcoming election; with such a danger in mind, the caucus, Fisk said, would feel constrained to withdraw its support of Madison and choose a more warlike candidate. Madison did not resist the "popular will."

Over the years since then, the weight of political reality has crushed, one by one, the frail hopes of the idealists among the Founding Fathers for the ineffable scheme they devised. If there remained a vestige of possibility that Electors might yet be chosen with an eye to their capacity to exercise superior judgment, it was made a mockery by the 1948 Electoral College of Michigan. Faced on their voting day with six vacancies in their ranks, the remaining thirteen Electors fell to the task, as prudence requires and the state law permits, of filling them. They descended to the streets of Lansing, rounded up half-a-dozen agreeable passers-by, and swore them in. Their qualifications? They belonged to the right party.

But we can still have it both ways. In that same year, 1948, one of Tennessee's eleven Electors, "appointed" by the Democratic voters, refused his vote to the Democratic candidate, Harry S. Truman; he gave it instead to the Dixiecrat candidate who had received only one-fourth as many votes as Mr. Truman. In Alabama eight years later, an Elector appointed on the ticket of Adlai E. Stevenson gave his vote to a local segregationist judge. Reminded of his party "loyalty oath" and his "moral duty," he replied, "I have fulfilled my obligations to the people of Alabama. I'm talking about the white people."

The Constitution was drafted by men who, when they wrote "We, the People," were also talking about the "white people"—not in the Alabaman's literal and contemptuous sense, but in the figurative and accustomed sense of the select. The franchise was largely confined to the propertied, and thus, in the context of the times, the better educated. This agrarian element was strong, and there, the Founders thought, power would remain in good hands.

That the United States would always be a small nation with a rural economy and a narrow suffrage—

on such a misconception was the new Constitution based. Some of the delegates believed they were creating a union which in time would inevitably disintegrate into its component states; their hope was that unity would last long enough to teach the states how to live together peaceably. Others were convinced that the republic must inescapably develop into a monarchy; their hope was that by the time it did, the people would have succeeded in establishing safeguards against too despotic a rule. The men of vision and good will held as firmly as they could to their principles. But, as Franklin explained while considering the document, "several parts" of which he confessedly disapproved: "When you assemble a number of men to have the advantage of their joint wisdom, you inevitably assemble with those men all their prejudices, their passions, their errors of opinion, their local interests, and their selfish views. . . ."

The passing years have aggravated the defects and anomalies of the Electoral College. The once-rural economy has given way to an intensively industrial order, great open spaces to surging metropolises. Large segments of the once-stationary populace have been forced into peripatetic pursuits; we are a nation on wheels. Places once weeks and months of arduous travel apart are now only minutes or hours away by air, split seconds away by ear or eye. And the suffrage is now all but universal. What was in 1787 "if not perfect at least excellent" seems to many in 1962 inequitable, illogical, and unjustifiable.

The selection of members of the Electoral College is based, to begin with, on certain mathematical inequities. Some of them are merely the result of the federal system. As each state, however small, has two senators (Nevada's 285,000 people wield as much power in the Senate as New York's 16,000,000) and has, in addition, at least one representative, it consequently has at least three Electors. Each of Alaska's three Electors in 1960 stood for fewer than 21,000 voters; each of New York's forty-five Electors represented more than 161,000 voters. This seems to make an Alaskan voter worth eight times a New Yorker. In practice, on the other hand, each New York voter appears to exert fifteen times the influence in the election—assuming that the Electors fulfill their "moral duty," and assuming also that the voter has voted for the winner in his state. For we come now to another bedeviling fact in the arrangement.

A candidate whose share of popular votes is one more than that of his nearest rival in any given state (though it may be, in a multiple contest, only a small minority of the total vote), receives all of that state's electoral votes—all his Electors have been "appointed."

This is the unit or winner-take-all system. In New York this meant in 1960 forty-five votes. (The new reapportionment has reduced it to forty-three.) A candidate who (by any slender margin) may win the electoral votes of New York and eleven other large states may become President even if—to carry the example to extremes—his opponent wins one hundred per cent of the popular *and* electoral votes of the other thirty-eight states.

Only in the rare instance—it hasn't happened since 1824—when the election falls to the House of Representatives (or the Senate for Vice President, which has occurred only once, in 1836) do the states have proportionate equality in the election of the Executive. Otherwise one candidate's tiny plurality in a large state may cancel out substantial blocs of votes for an opposing candidate in a number of smaller states.

But what about the substantial number of votes for the opposing candidate in the large state? In Illinois in the 1960 election, out of four and three quarter million votes, Mr. Kennedy received only 8,858 more than Mr. Nixon. Yet this infinitesimal plurality (it could have been only one, rather than 8,858) sufficed to "appoint" Mr. Kennedy's twenty-seven Electors. Two and a third million voters, it is sometimes argued, were thus in effect disfranchised. In reply, others hold that this is the fate of any minority, however large, in a democracy. But there is a rebuttal: the office at stake was not a state office. The President is the Chief Magistrate for all the people of the nation, wherever they may be. These more than two million votes for Mr. Nixon outweighed the Kennedy votes in half-a-dozen other states; would not justice demand that they be put in the balance?

Nor does it satisfactorily solve the problem to point out that for his part Mr. Nixon carried California's thirty-two electoral votes by a margin also calculable only in fractions of a percentage point. If chance must be relied on to offset inequities by counterbalancing inequities on the other side, chance may equally be counted on to heap all or most of them on one side. We might as well flip a coin, or choose our Presidents by lot (a proposal several times seriously made, and once endorsed by Chief Justice John Marshall).

Choice by lot is one of the quainter alternatives among a thousand or more proposals offered to our eighty-seven Congresses. The most seriously regarded systems fall generally into three main classes: 1) direct election of the Executive by the people at large, without regard to state lines; 2) election of the Electors by congressional districts, with two at large, in each state; 3) abolition of Electors and distribution of each state's electoral votes among the candidates in proportion to their respective shares of the state's popular vote.

Even the most ardent supporters of the first plan begin to despair of persuading small states (or large ones) to surrender the peculiar advantages they now enjoy. The third proposal has come closest to adoption in recent years. As the Lodge-Gosset amendment, it passed the Senate in 1950 with the required two-thirds majority, then died in the House. It was revived in 1956 by Senator Price Daniel of Texas with the impressive sponsorship of fifty-two other senators. To get it to the floor, he was forced in committee to accept a compromise proposal to let state legislatures, if they wished, adopt instead the congressional-district system.

How would each of these proposed systems have affected the outcome of the 1960 election?

If the Lodge-Gosset amendment had passed and been ratified by enough states in time for the 1960 election, the votes cast in that election, tallied by the new formula, would have given Kennedy only 266.070 electoral votes—three short of the absolute majority now required, but well above the forty per cent fixed as necessary for election in that amendment as ultimately refined. Nixon would have had 263.626. (Byrd would have received 3.118 and Faubus 2.756.)

Votes.	George Washington	John Adams	George Clinton	Thomas Jefferson	Aaron Burr
New-Hampshire, .	6	6			
Massachusetts, ..	16	16			
Rhode-Island, ..	4	4			
Connecticut, ...	9	9			
Vermont, :	3	3			
New-York, . , ..	12		12		
New-Jersey, . . .	7	7			
Pennsylvania, .	15	14	1		
Delaware, . . .	3	3			
Maryland. . ..	8	8			
Virginia, . . .	21.		21		
Kentucky, . .	.4			4	
North-Carolina, .	12		12		
South-Carolina, ..	8	7			1
Georgia, ...	4		4		
	133	77	50	4	1

As this page from the Senate Journal for 1793 shows, the Electors unanimously chose Washington for a second term, but split sharply over the Vice Presidency.

But the hypothesis contains its own possible invalidation. In certain one-party states, large numbers of opposition voters are known not to exert themselves to cast hopeless ballots, since the dominant party wins *all* the electoral votes in the state anyway. An end to the winner-take-all system might end the apathy. Although this would also affect Democratic voters in heavily Republican states, the "lost" G.O.P. vote may be larger. Nixon might have gotten the three additional electoral votes he needed to beat Kennedy.

Had the 1960 votes been tallied by the second system, election of the Electors by the then-existing congressional districts, a device whose latest exponent has been Senator Karl Mundt of South Dakota, Nixon would have won resoundingly: 279 to 244 (14 unpledged, but of no consequence since they could not affect the outcome). But the Mundt plan calls for division of each state into electoral districts of similar size with respect to population. This requirement would inhibit gerrymandering even more effectively than the recent federal court rulings on apportionment; we are again thrown back on speculation for the possible outcome.

The least probable of the current proposals—direct election of the President by the voters without regard to geographical boundaries—if applied to the 1960 figures would have given Mr. Kennedy the Presidency by 118,550 votes out of nearly 69 million.

Which system would have been the best gamble for the Democrats, if they had been able to make a choice before the 1960 election? Certainly the method of direct election looked dangerous: it was widely predicted that the popular vote would be very close. Assuming that no considerable number of Electors would depart from tradition and ignore the popular choice in their states, the old system of the Electoral College no doubt looked safest to the Kennedy camp, although as Election Day drew near it became ominously clear that at least some southern Electors would indeed disregard the tradition. The Lodge-Gosset system, despite its built-in advantages for the Republicans in the "solid south," at least would have protected the Democrats against the whims and vagaries of defecting Electors in the same region.

In view of this, there is some irony in the fact that the opposition that defeated the Lodge-Gosset amendment in 1956 was superbly led by the man who might four years later have been the victim of the anachronistic Electoral College—the junior (and freshman) senator from Massachusetts, John F. Kennedy. He skillfully led the attack that not only sent it back to committee, never again to emerge, but won away many of its sponsors.

Not the least interesting aspect of the debate was a seeming reversal of traditional attitudes. The crusade for change was pressed by conservatives of both parties; liberals on both sides of the aisle stood shoulder to shoulder against change. Defending status quo, liberal Senator Kennedy argued that no urgent necessity for alteration of the system had been proven. "No minority Presidents," he asserted, "have been elected in the twentieth century." (This was rather inaccurate, for Wilson in both his terms and Truman in 1948 had received less than half the popular vote.) "No elections have been thrown into the House of Representatives," Kennedy argued further, "no breakdown in the electoral system, or even a widespread lack of confidence in it, can be shown." Of course, that was four years before an Oklahoma Elector defected, and a governor and influential newspapers were inciting others to the same course, and an election involving Kennedy himself was won by 49.54 per cent of the popular vote over 49.09 per cent for the loser.

The restraints on the democratic process that stemmed from the Founding Fathers' distrust of the people are being trimmed away by the march of history. The first cut resulted from the power-pull that developed early between the Jeffersonian agrarian and the Hamiltonian mercantile interests. Each side sought to increase its strength by extending the voting prerogative to those in its sphere of influence formerly considered less deserving. Next came the leveling effect of rigorous frontier life in the newly opening western lands; the inevitable universal manhood suffrage spread its effects "back home." Since then, the Fourteenth, Fifteenth, Seventeenth, Nineteenth, and Twenty-third Amendments have vastly enlarged the rolls of those entitled in practice to exercise the sovereignty that all "the people" hold in theory. Finally, the Supreme Court decision in *Baker v. Carr*—the Tennessee reapportionment case—has led to a series of legislative and judicial moves that will further increase the balance of our voting system.

It is perhaps not too much to say, then, that in the foreseeable future yet another of the inequities imposed by archaic custom and the accident of state lines may be eliminated. The choice of their Chief Executive by the citizens of the *United* States will be by direct popular election—one voter, one vote, no matter where he may be on Election Day. Then the best man—at least in one meaningful sense—will always win.

Harry Louis Selden, for many years an editor and writer on foreign and domestic affairs, is vice chairman of the Fair Campaign Practices Committee, and a member of the National Committee for an Effective Congress.

For further reading: A History of Presidential Elections, by Eugene H. Roseboom (Macmillan, 1957).

Home, Mother, and the Flag;
humor, pathos, and bathos; the
lost look of Main Street fifty
years ago, in the heyday of the
horse and trolley—the old picture post card preserves it all

"Wish You Were Here"

By SANDER DAVIDSON

In the hierarchy of art collectors there are definite social strata as sacred as those of any ant colony. At the top, perhaps, belong the collectors of Chinese jades and oil paintings. Then come the fanciers of antique furniture, Dead Sea scrolls, and Baccarat paperweights. At the bottom of this social register languish the accumulators of cigar bands—and the picture post-card collectors. But if he is close to the lowest rung of the acquisitive society, unrecognized by the museums and Duveens, the post-card collector is nevertheless a kind of historian and, even if accidentally, serves a useful purpose.

The debut of the picture post card in the United States occurred at the Columbian Exposition of 1893. With its advent began a hobby and a collecting spree that whirled unabated until shortly after the First World War. Then suddenly the post-card album, a book second in importance only to the family Bible, vanished from atop the player piano.

At first, postal regulations permitted only the name and address of the recipient on the face of the card, so that of necessity messages defaced the illustrated side. In 1907, however, a key date to collectors, the Post Office Department relented: The faces of cards could be

To my Sweetheart

split down the middle to provide for address *and* message. This epochal decision saved the picture, unless, of course, you chose to mark X over some hotel window and label it "our room," or, "the body was found here." After 1907, therefore, the industry was off and running, and so was the hobby. While there were both artistic and trashy cards, sheer bulk was the general criterion of the collector—even when he was a specialist, devoted, say, only to cats, Santa Claus, or the Yerkes Observatory. (The writer once chanced upon a large album containing only views of prisons and cemeteries.) Ordinarily, though, not a traveler stirred from his bailiwick without being charged with the stern responsibility of mailing post cards of his travels to his album-keeping friends. This each person did gladly, for he knew the bread he cast upon the mail-box waters would return to him sevenfold. In turn the post-card publishers endeavored not only to sell cards embracing a variety of subjects but also to provide for the public a printed post card of charm and originality, often superbly colored, even embossed.

Indeed, post cards were much more than a means of communication; for more than twenty-five years they trace history, a kind of homely view of life in the United States, and in much of the civilized world. Often when no one else did, they recorded the landscape; it was a rare village green or country trolley-crossing that did not have its card. They celebrated Home, Mother, and the Flag; they helped out in courtship ("To the Candy Kid," or "Greetings to my Sweet Fluffy Ruffles"); they would Save Your Boy from the Saloon. They covered births, anniversaries, holidays (including Ground Hog Day), presidential candidates, burning issues like Prohibition and woman suffrage, heroes, smashing girls, fashions, sports, freaks (Frank Fithen the Armless Automobile Speed King), advertising, war (in its then-minor-league status), tragedies like the sinking of the *Maine* and the San Francisco earthquake, visiting royalty, celebrities of all kinds. Then there were cowboys, Indians, actors, actresses, expositions, fairs, parades, tender sentiments, anti-Semitica, erotica, jingoism, humor, pathos, and bathos. This is to say nothing of endless view cards depicting Old Faithful, Main Street everywhere, the Flat Iron Building, the fireproof steamer *Hustace B. Proxmire*, Lookout Mountain, the Hoosac Tunnel, and Lake Okoboji by moonlight.

To supply the insatiable demand, publishers sprang up like wildflowers. Frequently they had their pictures printed in Germany and Austria, where lithographic techniques were superior and painstaking workmanship very cheap. One of the more famous names in the postcard trade was the Detroit Publishing Company, with almost 16,000 different views taken for it by photographers who traveled all over the country. Many of the company's cards are models of color, composition, and meticulous detail. Edward H. Mitchell was the largest western company, and other large manufacturers included L. J. Koehler (publisher of "Hold-to-the-Light" cards), Winsch, Art Publishing, and Rotograph. Bamforth and Company and Raphael Tuck and Sons, the leading English firms, exported many delightful cards made expressly for the American market. The German publisher Stengel and the Italian firm of Sborgi set the picture post-card standard for reproductions of fine art.

Like so many other simpler things, the early post card fell victim, after the First World War, to the new era of sophistication and mass production. That album seemed, suddenly, so old-fashioned. And nowadays, a few decades later, you can get a card, if you want to save writing a letter, that looks like—and indeed may be—a perfect color photograph. Yet something, somehow, is lacking: craftsmanship, perhaps, or a sense of the past, the warm moment of charm or surprise that one might, only a few decades ago, bestow on another for the price of the card and a penny stamp.

MAIN STREET

PEORIA, ILL. Adams Street, Looking North.

2555—
Main St.,
Looking
South,
Hartford,
Conn.

[handwritten message]

...venir Post Card Co., New York and Berlin.

Houston Street. San Antonio, Tex.

COPR. DETROIT PUBLISHING CO.

12614 FRONT ST., MARQUETTE, MICH.

Main Street. Looking East. Oklahoma City, Okla.

The most popular of all post cards showed Main Street—even if it were called State, or Congress, or Washington—because it made clear you were there. It might not yet be paved, but several views of it were offered. How different the store fronts look today, how utterly vanished the ubiquitous trolley! Cards like these provide a graphic record, often the only one left, of the growth of our towns into cities.

GARFIELD MEMORIAL.

CLEVELAND. OHIO.

Dear Etta was in this tomb yesterday It is Garfield's It is all marble and simply handsome I have a few more beads Well I must close. with love Sadie

Band Concert. Soldiers Home. Milwaukee, Wis.

"Having Wonderful Time"

10552   A SOUTHERN BAPTISM

The post-card sleuth would know at a glance that the "Garfield Memorial" post card was published prior to 1907 because of the message space on the card's front. More gumshoeing would reveal that it is a private mailing-card authorized by an Act of Congress in 1898. But we shall never find out about Sadie's beads. The same expert would quickly recognize "A Southern Baptism" as a product of the Detroit Publishing Co., with the 10,000 series and the divided face telling him it was published in 1907. Below: singeing a corner *proved* you had really been to the volcano.

Troop of Cavalry on a fallen big Tree, California.

195. Tourists Scorching Post Cards, Volcano of Kilauea, Hawaiian Islands.

The cry for help.

The Rescue.

At last this hero draws quite near, she stretches out her arm,
"Fear not, he cries, dear little maid, I'll save you from all harm."

Saved.

He lifts her then close to his breast, and slowly he goes down.
The people in the street below, all breathless stand around.

Rewarding the rescuer.

CARDBOARD HEROES

Once upon a time there was a world full of simpler dangers than the ones we know today, and cards like these recall it. They were intended to be utterly serious, an apostrophe to the chivalrous fireman, a cheer for the bold soldier boy, his mouth full of unimpeachable, if ill-spelt, sentiments completely satisfying to both sender and recipient. There were thousands of patriotic cards; you could save them for the Fourth, or for Memorial Day, or use them every day.

I love thee, dear sweet home and I
Will stick to thee, and when I die
My fellowmen with heart and blood —
My take my place — I know they would!

546—Cherrelyn Horse Car, Denver

DOUBLE DECK BUS, ON FIFTH AVENUE, NEW YORK CITY.

WHEELS & WINGS

Three Great Trunk Lines Crossing at Richmond, Va.

View from the rea

Aunt

Post cards covered the romantic period of the river steamer, the foolproof biplane, and the steam cars. Who is that vision in white on the Road of Anthracite? Could it be Phoebe Snow? Who else? They also saluted more prosaic modes of travel like the open-air Fifth Avenue bus and the Cherrelyn public tram, which operated on the fair-play principle: it carried the horse downhill if he would pull the car up.

nd of the Lackawanna Limited. The Daylight Flyer over the road of Anthracite.

this lovely Mrs Roufals

KELLY FIELDS. SAN ANTONIO. TEX.

FOOL PROOF BIPLANE STARTING OFF ON A FLIGHT.

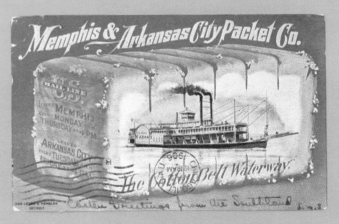

Memphis & Arkansas City Packet Co.

The Cotton Belt Waterway.

THE TWINS.

MISS AMERICA

ENNSYLVANIA

Does this make your heart go pit-a-pat?
Marion

SOFT EYES, BIG HATS

Is everyone sure that girls are prettier now than when these cards were turned out? It was the day of the Christy Girl, the Gibson Girl, big hats, and illusions. Two of the cards shown here, opposite and above left, are the exquisite work of Philip Boileau. The schoolgirls of Paris (Texas, alas!) are somewhat fraudulent: the same faces appeared on "high-school cards" from many other cities. You just changed the name and the building. The college girl also shifted allegiance with fickle frequency.

High School Building, Paris, Texas.

Pretty girls, pretty girls everywhere, But the PARIS BELLES are claimed most fair.

SENTIMENT & SENTIMENTALITY

In the world of the post card, all emotions were oversimplified: sentiment was gooey, morality hard-hitting, and humor as broad as the waistcoat of William Howard Taft. The only things gooier or broader, perhaps, are the so-called "sentimentals" which you can still find today at any cheap newsstand. Verses, songs, pious observations, and pledges against liquor and tobacco (many with space provided for signatures) were available in an infinite variety of bad taste we can only hint at here. Yet if the gem of birchbark rococo on the opposite page seems to reach a new low, it is worth remembering that it may—who knows?— have speeded some faltering courtship.

If I only knew how to begin.-

11205 Tee-We-Lee-Ma, the last living descendant of Massasoit, whose friendship and generosity saved the Pilgrims from starvation

PHOTO ONLY COPYRIGHTED BY F. W. GLASIER 1906.

The Likeness
of Fame

BILL TAFT AND H

BROTHER CHARLEY

OLYMYMPIA

MATA-HARI

The passing post-card parade took cognizance
of all kinds of notable people, whether important or
merely freakish. The motion-picture newsreel had
scarcely appeared, and few magazines or newspapers
offered the public vivid likenesses of the
personalities who molded their destiny or aroused
their curiosity. This task, long ago, was performed to
no small degree by cards, which also offered magical
color, if not always flattery. During all presidential
campaigns from 1898 to 1918, picture post cards
of the nominees were mailed at a furious rate.
Stage and film stars aware of the publicity value
inherent in a penny post card also used it to promote
themselves. A choice example of this approach is the
French card above of Mata Hari, who later went on
to a bigger if more hazardous career. Here
she is seen as an entertainer before becoming
a famous spy during the First World War.

Storm King, Hudson River (from the South)

DAY INTO NIGHT

Walker Evans, writing in *Fortune,* has said of post cards that "on their tinted surfaces were some of the truest visual records ever made of any period." As our contributor John Ripley points out by way of footnote, truth sometimes suffered at the hands of thrifty card makers. In this pair, for example, one publisher's retoucher has transformed another's daylight scene (above) into the explosive "sunset" below. It was done all the time, but in the larger sense, for all the trickery, Walker Evans was very right.

Storm King, Hudson River, N.Y.